# Limitless

Discover the Fullness of God's Kingdom in Your Life

Anthony S. Ramsey

 renownpublishing

**Renown Publishing**
**www.renownpublishing.com**

**Limitless / Anthony S. Ramsey**
ISBN-13: 978-1-952602-10-8

# CONTENTS

# Foreword by Bishop Andrew Merritt

One of the most profound things in the universe is the unlimited availability of a loving God. There is nothing, and I mean nothing, more potent or secure than having an intimate encounter with the inexhaustible attributes found in the majesty of God as Father and Jesus as Deliverer.

We are experiencing a shortage of people who have experienced His love in this measure. Although it is available to all who are willing to surrender to the supremacy of the Lord's nature, many live stuck in the bondages of fear, absent the presence of faith.

I can recall having a conversation with my son, Anthony, after he had preached his first message in our church. When we were alone later that afternoon, I asked him, "Where did you get that message from?" He responded, "God gave it to me." I smiled and said to him, "If God gave you that message, then you will have to live every word that you just preached."

Today, I can say without reservation that the message he preached that day became the syllabus for his life of faith. I can tell you that he learned the limitless power of

God through every step of his journey. Of course, it wasn't always easy. Yes, I had to watch with a heavy heart at times. But I have always been fully confident that the God in him would manifest Himself in every lesson, conditioning him to pass every test.

In his new book, *Limitless: Discover the Fullness of God's Kingdom in Your Life*, Anthony challenges us to remove the boundaries that have been placed in our lives and to lean into all possibilities.

Don't hold yourself back any longer. It's time to live the life that God desires to release in you by faith, today!

In the Yoke of the Master,

Bishop Andrew Merritt

PREFACE

# Living What We Preach

Before you skip this section and jump to Chapter One, I ask you to pause and allow me to share a bit of my story with you. In the next few pages of this preface, I share some personal insights into my life and the things that I, my family, and Kingdom Living Church have experienced. These experiences give weight to the message in this book. I want you to know and understand that God will see you through. Deliverance isn't always His answer. He doesn't always utilize the miraculous. He's after growth in you—growth in faith and awareness of His presence when you can't feel Him. Keep moving forward when nothing around you says, *"God."* Know He's with you. Don't let anything move you except the Word of God.

My wife Marvella and I celebrated thirty years of marriage on August 5, 2019. Where has all the time gone? As I reflect on our lives together and all the tremendous blessings of God's favor, along with things we've suffered through in the service of God, I marvel at His faithfulness to us and our children, Rosston, Ria, and Roman.

We had no idea what God had in store for us when my grandmother Bethola Fair took Marvella, who was my girlfriend at the time, and me to Straight Gate Church in Detroit. Marvella and I had no idea we would spend the next twenty-plus years of our lives at that church, faithfully following our leaders—Bishop Andrew and Pastor Viveca Merritt—serving people, learning ministry, developing our faith, and ultimately receiving the call to ministry.

During this timeframe, both Marvella and I experienced success in our corporate careers. My twenty-five-year career as an automotive executive culminated in me becoming chief executive officer and manufacturing director of an automotive supplier. In addition, I was later unanimously elected to the company's board of directors. It appeared the next step for me was as company president and possibly a stake in ownership. Marvella's fifteen-year career in higher education culminated in her position as a senior compliance officer of finance for charter schools for a prominent university. By 2005, we were living in a five-thousand-square-foot home and our children were in private schools. Life was good.

Then drastic changes happened in quick succession. In October 2006, I informed my employer that I was founding a church. Three months later, Bishop and Pastor Viveca laid hands on us, and we were installed as pastors. Kingdom Living Church (KLC) was born with five members: me, Marvella, and our three children. We held our first service at a local elementary school in Grand Blanc, Michigan.

In March 2008, I was called to the office to meet with the company president and was told it was my last day. I had to turn in my company car and credit cards within twenty-four hours. My insurances were to be terminated in thirty days, and there would be no severance pay. So, in March 2008, by faith, we went into full-time ministry. In addition to our Sunday and midweek services, I started a local radio show on Saturdays.

In August 2009, the housing market collapse gutted the value of our home. We owed more than the house was worth, and we ultimately lost our home in foreclosure. I wasn't bringing in any income outside of unemployment. Kingdom Living was not in a position to pay me any compensation. We began to grow; however, we never told our congregation or our families what we were going through. We simply trusted God to provide a place for us.

During this time, Marvella was diagnosed with multiple sclerosis. There is no known cure for MS. I remember when we met with the head of neurology and he showed us the MRI results. We could see she had at least eight lesions on her brain and spine. She was experiencing multiple symptoms throughout her body. The doctor informed us that the best he could offer was a host of medicines, through daily injections, that could possibly slow the progression of the disease but not cure it. The injections averaged about $3,000 to $4,000 per month.

After the doctor gave his diagnosis, I thanked him for his efforts, but I told him, "We are people of faith." Right in his office, I grabbed his hand and began to pray, declaring my wife's healing of multiple sclerosis. In spite of the reality of the doctor's diagnosis, we deemed the Word of God greater.

Meanwhile, as we continued to believe God, KLC continued to grow, and we went from our original location at Andersen Elementary School to a small but beautiful suite in an office building.

There's a supernatural story behind the location in that office building. The suite was newly leased to another tenant. The lease was signed. God spoke to Marvella and asked her if we wanted that location. We both told God yes. We went back to inquire about the suite a few days later and discovered that the new tenant had suddenly backed out of the lease. Supernaturally, God was making a way for Kingdom Living Church.

It was here that we began to mature as a ministry. We would experience the supernatural hand of God throughout our time in the office building. After three years, our lease was up and God led me not to re-sign it— He had something better. By not signing the lease, I understood there was a risk someone else could lease the property. Without knowing where God was leading us, I informed our landlord we would not renew the lease, and he promptly signed a new tenant.

Now we had to be out in sixty days, with no idea of our next step. However, my wife and I understood God is our provider. I remember, I kept thinking, *"But—God!"* When you trust Him, you are not at risk. He had a place for us. I just didn't know where yet.

God led me to a local real-estate agent, who just happened to be a Spirit-filled believer. After a few weeks, I received a call from the agent. He said, "Pastor, I found your new church building. It's on seventeen acres centrally located off the expressway." I went to see the property that day. I couldn't believe it! I'd driven by the property a hundred times and never noticed it. It was a run-down lumber yard. It was overrun with weeds, flooded, infested with racoons and every other critter you could think of.

When I got out of my car and my feet touched the ground, I heard the voice of God in my heart. I heard with my spiritual ear, "This is the place I have for you!" I was overwhelmed with emotion. To the unspiritual eye, this was a dump. But to me, this was the new church campus for Kingdom Living Church. I believed it would one day include a five-thousand-seat auditorium, a recreation center, a health clinic, an outdoor amphitheater, and a school. I saw it. I felt it in my spirit.

In October 2011, we signed a five-year lease agreement that included a first right of refusal clause. We leased the property from a West Coast company worth over $20 billion. At this time, KLC had roughly forty members.

The township had condemned the run-down old lumber yard as uninhabitable, but by faith, over the next three years, we transformed the property to a beautiful facility. We did $400,000 worth of renovations—all in cash, without any debt. We never instituted a building fund. God simply moved on the hearts of people through tithes and offerings. There were many instances of supernatural giving by people to whom God spoke.

We revamped all the lighting, heating, cooling, and floors. We put in HVAC, plumbing, new AC units, bathrooms, and water heaters. We built a café, added a bookstore, and overhauled the floor plan. We added carpet, painted, laid ceramic flooring, built a stage, put marble in the sanctuary, and so forth. We laid out a clear vision, and people sowed into the vision in faith. People saw the transformation happening right before their eyes.

The ministry grew substantially in two years. The owners of the property were extremely supportive and donated $17,000 to help us with our vision. The landlord's representatives indicated their interest to help us purchase the property at the end of our lease.

We saw the hand of God time and time again. I believed God spoke to me that this was the place He had chosen for KLC. We believed this was our wealthy place. We witnessed healings, financial miracles, and favor almost continuously. We witnessed people being healed from cancer and various other diseases. We got all our bookstore furniture from a local bookstore that went out of business. We got an entire security camera system from a Blockbuster video store that had gone out of business. Everything was first-rate for pennies on the dollar. Our church services and events flourished. From this base of operations, we were able to start evangelistic ministries in the local jail, at a homeless shelter in Flint, Michigan, and in a regional state prison.

Then everything changed. Halfway through our lease, the management team of our landlord changed. All the people we worked with for the first two years were removed. The supportive relationship changed to a combative relationship overnight. We put together a formal offer to buy the property midway through the lease, but our offer was rejected.

By the end of our lease, the property was listed for roughly one million dollars. Our renovation had increased the property value from uninhabitable to $1,000,000. A number of possible buyers visited the property. We suspected an offer had been made. We made another offer to purchase, and the seller never responded to us. We suspected the seller had an offer that they intended to accept; however, we were never given the opportunity to match the offer per the first right of refusal clause in our lease. From our perspective, it looked as though the seller merely intended to allow our lease to expire without giving us an opportunity to review the offer we believed they had in hand.

From here, a three-year legal battle ensued. We refused to leave the property. They sued to evict us. This was truly a David versus Goliath story. The Associated Press picked up the story. We appeared on local TV and radio to bring attention to our case.

For the next two-and-a-half years, through district court, circuit court, and later, the court of appeals, we waged a legal war, all the while believing God was with us. We hired two of the best attorneys possible and laid out an aggressive legal strategy to validate our claim that our lease was violated by the landlord's intention not to give Kingdom Living Church the right to match a secretive offer they had received prior to the conclusion of our lease. This was the basis of our case, and everything hinged on us proving they had an offer they intended to accept.

The company that opposed us was a large West Coast conglomerate worth billions. Their wealth, prestige, and reputation were then, and are still today, well respected in the marketplace. I hold no ill will against them or their leadership personally. This confrontation came down to what I believe God said to me and our courage to stand up for our legal rights as tenants in the eyes of the law.

Based on this experience, I can better relate to the stories and sacrifices of many of the faith heroes chronicled in Hebrews 11. When God speaks to you, His voice is simply irresistible. The attraction of His presence in the storm overwhelms the power of those who oppose you.

Looking back on this experience now, I realize this chapter in my life had been foretold ten years prior by my spiritual father, Bishop Andrew Merritt. I remember it like it was yesterday. I preached my first sermon at Straight Gate Church. Afterward, my bishop called me to his office. I assumed I must have said something wrong and he was going to correct me. I was nervous while I waited for him to call me into his office.

He called me in and asked me a strange question: "Where did you get that sermon?" I was more than a little perplexed. I responded, "God gave it to me." He paused— and then prophesied, "You will have to walk out everything you preached tonight." That was it.

At that time, I had no idea the magnitude of those words, but looking back, I see that the battle with our landlord was unavoidable. KLC was predestined for this confrontation. This was the devil's plan to ensure KLC would never survive to fulfill its purpose to transform the Grand Blanc Genesee County region for Jesus Christ. Now I see it as the cross we—my wife, our children, the KLC family, and I—were chosen to bear. Like Joseph, whom the Word of the Lord tried until the time when his word came (see Psalm 105:17–22), by faith we paid the price for victory.

Now, I'm sure many of you reading this book would ask, "Why not just walk away? Maybe this wasn't God's will for you. There's no way you can defeat a foe with a recorded net worth of over $20 billion, who could hire the best law firms in the country" (which they did).

The answer to that question is what this book is about—relationship with God. When you believe God has spoken to you, the depth of the relationship gives you the courage to take on any foe, no matter how powerful. Moses took on Pharaoh, David took on Goliath, Elijah took on Ahab and Jezebel. It's not the size of the foe that matters; it's the size of God in your eyes. I trusted God through the legal process. I learned to trust God when we got good news and when the news was bad. My relationship with God sustained me when my endurance had long given out.

This legal battle included over twenty individual hearings and all the costs associated with it. We hired one of the best firms in the state to represent us. We never asked for pro bono assistance. Our stance was, *"If God ordained it, He will pay for it,"* and He did.

At the end of this journey, I found out from the opposing legal team that they thought we were getting pro bono legal assistance. They couldn't understand how a small church with a small congregation could put up the kind of legal fight we put up. I remember vividly at the last hearing I attended, the lead attorney for the opposition shook my hand and said he had the utmost respect for our church and for me and for how we conducted ourselves.

You see, even in an intense legal battle, we never wrote a mean-spirited email or had a heated phone conversation. I was always polite and respectful, irrespective of how I felt we were being treated. We maintained our integrity throughout.

The judge at the circuit court was, in our legal team's view, particularly aggressive against our case. We sought legal due process to go before a jury of our peers to decide the case, but we experienced a judge who had an apparent strong leaning toward big business. It seemed like the entire atmosphere of the courtroom changed whenever our case came up. In several hearings, the proceedings were calm and efficient until it was time for our case; then, the judge became emotional and, on two occasions, singled me out as unintelligent and a questionable leader for agreeing to our lease.

I remember telling Bishop Merritt, who accompanied me to several of our hearings, that this judge was an unjust judge just like in the Bible (Luke 18). We kept coming before him and laying out our case. In the final hearing, we felt like we had the momentum to get our case to trial. The judge legally was now in position to allow a jury to decide who was right. This was the worst-case scenario for our opponent: a huge West Coast-based corporation trying to destroy a church in Grand Blanc (near Flint), Michigan, at the height of the water contamination disaster. I was so confident! Our legal team was already planning to prep me on how to take the stand and give testimony.

Around that time, I went on a two-day fast. I went to a local hotel to shut myself away for prayer, listening for God's voice. The day after my fast, I got a phone call. It was the president and CEO of our opponent. It's not every day when the president of a $20 billion company calls you personally. We had a very pleasant conversation, and he gave me his personal cell phone number to call him back to discuss a settlement option. And although we couldn't come to an agreement, I appreciated his efforts and realized more than ever that God was with us. A small church in Grand Blanc with a few hundred members had wrestled with a large money market giant and forced them to the negotiating table.

However, the judge ruled against us: he denied us the right to a jury trial. To say I was crushed and despondent is an understatement. I was in too much pain to be angry in the days that followed. I asked God why but received no answer. I analyzed my motives and actions, and checked and rechecked my decisions. No answer came, only extreme frustration. I wondered if I had missed God. How could this happen? The devil said to me, *"You missed God, and your days as a pastor are over. Quit. The saints are going to abandon KLC. You are a failure. God was never with you. If He had been, the judge would've ruled in your favor."*

I remember telling God, *"I'm done. I'm going to bed and I don't want to wake up in the morning. Just take me. I trusted You and somehow, someway I missed You. You're God, so there's no point in blaming you. It's me. It's all my fault."*

I cannot put into words the faith and strength of my wife, Pastor Marvella. As I reflect on this timeframe, I recall that her faith never wavered. She never second-guessed my decisions. She stood by me and encouraged me greatly throughout the entire ordeal, as only a soul mate could.

We appealed and won on one of the three counts. In spite of the ruling, God was at work behind the scenes.

At the time, a family member worked at a circuit court in another county. During the previous three years, I had never shared any of the court proceedings with anyone in my family. He knew the ministry had open litigation, but he knew none of the details or issues. Just after the Christmas season, in passing, he asked me the name of the judge in our case. I told him the name, and he said, "I thought that was his name. You know, he stepped down from the bench abruptly. He's no longer a judge."

I was floored. As an officer of the court, he couldn't tell me any details, but apparently, the judge had engaged in some inappropriate behavior. The judge abruptly retired. The unjust judge's case appeared before my family member's judge. God, who is our judge and law-giver, controls everything. He rules over every court system. God changed the court's docket of cases to bring His justice! So it's not a coincidence that the unjust judge's case ended up before my family member's judge.

In short, the circuit court judge who ruled against us had hastily retired within sixty days of his ruling against us. The judge was young and at the height of his powers, but he mistreated KLC, God's people. I believe the Holy Spirit enacted vengeance against this judge. God said in His Word that vengeance belongs to Him. I believe this is exactly what happened.

God is amazing. We ended up renting a small building across town. Every time I drove to our new location, I had to drive past the old location, 16.4 acres of land right off the expressway. To and from church, I would see our old location, and the devil would rub it in my face. It turns out the company that bought the property after our eviction was the same company that we suspected our landlord had a deal with prior to the end of our lease. They tore down the building on the property that we had renovated, wiping away any trace that a church had ever been on the premises.

Then, several months later, as I drove home from Sunday, God spoke to me so clearly, it was as though I heard Him audibly. God said, "You didn't lose. The property was a seed!"

In that instant, my entire life changed. The property was a seed that had to be sown. What had been prophesied by a man of God, all those years before, had been fulfilled.

*Verily, verily, I say unto you, except a corn of wheat fall into the ground and die, it abideth alone: but if it die, it bringeth forth much fruit.*

—*John 12:24*

Our harvest is on the way. Every dollar, every prayer, every sacrifice, every embarrassment and insult to our integrity is being restored. God is showing us that He is a rewarder. We ultimately settled with our opponent. The law firm wrote off a significate amount of our legal fees. The ministry is debt-free. We just kept moving forward. A lot of wonderful people left the ministry, but those who remained with us after the eviction and court proceedings understand how Daniel endured the lion's den and how the three Hebrews went into and came out of the fiery furnace.

The leadership of KLC never wavered. I never mentioned the details of the legal events from the pulpit at any time. As a matter of fact, I never said anything to anyone except for a select team of people. As a result, during this three-year period, KLC never wavered in its mission to be a light to the region and world for Jesus Christ. We led more people to Jesus during that timeframe than at any point in our church's history. God opened effectual doors to preach in the local jail, homeless shelter, and federal prison in our region.

The ministry is flourishing. We have people who are battle-tested, who chose to stay where God planted them. They've been taught you can only grow where God plants you. We ordained six amazing people as ministers last year alone. Our vision has been tested and has triumphed. KLC continues to move forward in its God-given assignment in the world. Our mission statement will one day touch the four corners of the earth: "Kingdom Living Church: where it's not about religion but relationship."

INTRODUCTION

# It's About Relationship

The Holy Spirit has inspired me to write this book to awaken your awareness of the danger that lurks in and around our churches—a danger that invades our homes, our families, and our marriages. It's the one danger that, if left unchecked, will at first exhaust and ultimately bankrupt your God-given authority on earth.

If you assumed that I'm referring to the devil, you're mistaken. Jesus, through His life, death, and resurrection, completely destroyed Satan's power of sin and death over mankind. All power in heaven and on the earth and beneath the earth is in Jesus' hands (Philippians 2:10). The entire universe has been purged of Satan's rulership. Now you are truly free. Whom the Son sets free is free indeed (John 8:36).

If you are a believer, any notion or impulse that designates you as a sinner saved by grace is in error, demonic, and part of Satan's feeble attempt to enslave a freed person. Once you become born again, you are no longer a sinner but a saint. You are seated in Christ, freed from the bondage of sin and death. Satan's hold on your life has been completely destroyed by the power of Jesus' resurrection. You no longer relate to sin; therefore, it is incorrect to designate yourself as a sinner. The power of sin has been completely destroyed in your life. As you read the following scripture, understand that it highlights the thoroughness of Satan's defeat:

> *He canceled out every legal violation we had on our record and the old arrest warrant that stood to indict us. He erased it all—our sins, our stained soul—he deleted it all and they cannot be retrieved! Everything we once were in Adam has been placed onto his cross and nailed permanently there as a public display of cancellation.*
>
> *Then Jesus made a public spectacle of all the powers and principalities of darkness, stripping away from them every weapon and all their spiritual authority and power to accuse us. And by the power of the cross, Jesus led them around as prisoners in a procession of triumph. He was not their prisoner; they were his!*
>
> *—Colossians 2:14–15 (TPT)*

The absoluteness of Jesus' victory over Satan rules out the devil as the danger I'm referring to. Let me give you a clue about whom or what I'm referring to. Dictionary.com defines danger as "liability or exposure to harm or injury; risk; peril."[1]

Jesus warned His disciples of the present peril that threatened the effectiveness of God's kingdom in their lives:

> *Then Jesus said unto them, Take heed and beware of the leaven of the Pharisees and of the Sadducees. ... Then understood they how that he bade them not beware of the leaven of bread, but of the doctrine of the Pharisees and of the Sadducees.*
>
> *—Matthew 16:6, 12*

Look carefully at the two aforementioned scriptures.

Jesus is warning the disciples to beware of the doctrines being taught and espoused by the religious leaders of his day. Notice Jesus didn't say anything about the devil or about falling into sin. I personally believe our obsession with a defeated devil and fear of sin has taken our eyes off the real danger lurking in plain sight—religion. Or, as Jesus referred to it, the doctrine of the Pharisees and the Sadducees.

Consider the etymology of the word *religion*. This word likely originated from the Latin *religio*, meaning "obligation, bond, reverence," or possibly from the Latin *religare,* meaning "to bind."[2] At its essence, religion binds us. Jesus, however, sets us free.

Satan is defeated, but religion is alive and well. We see it in today's headlines. A follower of some radical form of Islam straps a bomb to his body, goes into a market filled with innocent women and children, and detonates the bomb, killing himself and as many people as possible. What was his motivation? What was he thinking as he pushed the detonator? Why was there so little regard for others that even innocent children weren't spared? Those who sponsored his death tell you openly it was all done in the name of their religion.

Violence and oppression in the name of religion doesn't discriminate; it occurs in every religion and in every century. Consider:

- Thousands of people were tortured and murdered during the Spanish Inquisition in the name of God and religion.

- Protestant and Catholic battled for supremacy in the streets of Northern Ireland for much of the twentieth century based primarily along religious lines.

- Recently, the nation of Sudan was divided in

half—one half Christian and the other Islamic.

- After the second Gulf War, we saw the headline news showing gun battles between Sunni and Shiite.

Moreover, while it may not involve the loss of life, we see the lines of division in the Christian faith between different denominations: Lutheran, Methodist, Baptist, Southern Baptist, Apostolic, Pentecostal, non-denominational, and so on. These groups all profess Jesus as Lord, yet rarely interact, seldom collaborate, and assume the other groups as doctrinally insufficient to some degree. The people belonging to these denominations all claim the Bible is the inerrant Word of God, and yet they are uniquely separate. I'm not for or against any denomination, and I respect each for its respective contribution to the body of Christ; however, I believe the origin of this great divide is in religion.

Matthew 24:6 speaks of wars and rumors of wars. I believe these wars will take place along religious lines. History is preparing to repeat itself, only on an unimaginable scale of death and destruction.

We used to feel somewhat safe. These stories of violence were reported to us from abroad, from a distant land, and they were about people we didn't know. However, now these stories happen in our cities, neighborhoods, schools, and churches.

Religion—the doctrine of the Pharisees and the Sadducees—is the greatest threat to God's people. Religion threatens to enslave, frustrate, and disarm believers of their covenant rights and privileges. The Bible states that the gates of hell cannot prevail against the true church (Matthew 16:18); however, Satan has opposed us in a strategy to corrupt our understanding of the Word of God, dulling its power through a false form of godliness

(2 Timothy 3:5), denying the inherent authority every believer must possess if he or she is to dominate in the earth.

What is the answer? What is our response to the proliferation of religion invading the church? Where are the proofs, power, and authority Jesus said we would demonstrate after His ascension (Acts 1:8)? Why are so many believers anointed but frustrated, giving but lacking, believing but not manifesting?

These are all reasonable questions that deserve answers. I will attempt to provide those answers in this book. Just like you, I had many of the same questions, and I was desperate for answers. What I have uncovered has changed my life, and I'm hopeful this knowledge will alter the course of your life, too.

Lack of knowledge is one of our greatest vulnerabilities:

> *My people are destroyed for lack of knowledge: because thou hast rejected knowledge, I will also reject thee, that thou shalt be no priest to me: seeing thou hast forgotten the law of thy God, I will also forget thy children.*
> **—Hosea 4:6**

Ignorance of God's Word is your greatest opponent in life. What you don't know can kill you and negatively impact future generations. Whether this book helps you a little or a lot, I pray to the Father that the mysteries of the kingdom of heaven resonate in your heart and mind. Matthew 13:11 makes it clear you have a right to obtain insight into the deep things of God.

The chapters of this book are designed to enhance your thirst and love for the truth of His Word and to help you grow in your faith. I've also included two appendixes at the end of the book as practical supplements to encourage you in your walk: an overview of God's plan for humanity and life lessons to be learned from Abraham.

God is willing to give you what you ask, reveal what you seek, and open the door that gives you access. I believe it's your time to experience a rediscovery of clarity of kingdom dominion and the manifestation of His promises.

The Holy Spirit has revealed the Father's passion to give you the kingdom, the same kingdom of heaven prepared for you before the foundation of the world (Ephesians 1:4). As you read this book, use your faith to unlock the kingdom authority within you.

Yours in the bonds of Christ,
Pastor Anthony S. Ramsey

CHAPTER ONE

# Removing the Tares

A hunger and thirst for God's righteousness motivated me to write this book. Like many believers, I have experienced God's blessing in so many areas of my life: marriage, family, health, career, and ministry. Time and time again, God has shown Himself strong on my behalf. By biblical standards, I am a blessed man.

However, I noticed areas in my life that appeared stagnant, unproductive, and unfruitful. When I compared His promises to my current state, it forced me to be honest with myself and ask, "Why do some areas of my life flourish while others remain unchanged? I know the Word of God is perfect, inerrant, and all-encompassing. I know God loves me and only wants the best for me!"

Then I encountered, in a fresh way, the following words of Jesus:

*Another parable put he forth unto them, saying, The kingdom of heaven is likened unto a man which sowed good seed in his field: But while men slept, his enemy came and sowed tares among the wheat, and went his way. But when the blade was sprung up, and brought forth fruit, then appeared the tares also. So the servants of the*

*householder came and said unto him, Sir, didst not thou*
*sow good seed in thy field? from whence then hath it tares?*
*He said unto them, An enemy hath done this. The servants*
*said unto him, Wilt thou then that we go and gather them*
*up?*

—*Matthew 13:24–28*

*Webster's Dictionary 1828 Edition* defines *tare* as "a weed of grain fields especially of biblical times that is usually held to be the darnel."[3] In other words, a tare is a weed that grows in the midst of a farmer's harvest. If left unchecked, the tares will grow alongside the harvest and will eventually choke out the harvest.

I began to understand that the kingdom of heaven in me had detected a small virus called *religion* that the enemy had somehow planted in my thinking. And even though I had experienced many victories in my life, there was still the presence of a few tares—not enough to choke out the harvest but enough to be a nuisance. Enough to get my attention. Enough to desire to be completely free.

It's like having malware on your computer. Your computer still works but it's slow. It's easy to get complacent with a slow computer. You develop work-arounds that allow you to still use it, but it's frustrating.

That's where a lot of believers find themselves. Saved but frustrated. Blessed but still in need. Believing the Word but desperate for a breakthrough.

## *Two Kinds of Seed*

If you're anything like me, you need an answer, a biblical truth that helps bring some rationale to what you're going through and concludes in victory. The answer I received was buried in the wheat and tares parable that Jesus taught. I began to understand that the enemy sows seeds, too. However, when revelation from

God comes, all satanic delays are destroyed, dreams come true, and destinies are fulfilled.

*When hope's dream seems to drag on and on, the delay can be depressing. But when at last your dream comes true, life's sweetness will satisfy your soul.*

**—Proverbs 13:12** *(TPT)*

Many believers attend multiple church services each week—usually a midweek service and a Sunday worship service. Each time the minister teaches or preaches a sermon, he or she is depositing the seed of God's Word in your mind. Over time, and through repetition and personal study, the sown Word penetrates into your heart. The Holy Spirit uses that Word to speak to you and through you in accordance with His will. It's important to note that the instant the Word is heard, you possess the faith needed for the manifestation of what the Word promises. Faith comes by hearing (Romans 10:17). When you hear the Word, faith comes instantly, not by feeling but by hearing. I'm being redundant because many people want to feel something to confirm their faith. Feeling is a resource of your flesh. Faith, on the other hand, is an operation of the Spirit. Therefore, the sowing of the Word is fundamental to all spiritual growth.

However, the enemy is sowing his word, too. Every time you turn on your TV, use your computer, watch a movie, engage social media, or utilize any other information platform, the enemy is sowing tares.

Jesus tells us to take heed to what we hear (Mark 4:24). Somewhere along the line a seed was sown that opposes the truth. The enemy sowed a lie to distort or destroy the truth. Maybe it was music. Maybe it was hanging with the wrong crowd. Maybe it was watching something that the Holy Spirit warned you not to watch. Somewhere, somehow, something got in, laid dormant for a season, but one day sprouted up seemingly out of nowhere. The enemy did this.

Satan is subtle. He manifests himself as an angel of light (2 Corinthians 11:14). He knows you are far too intelligent for his invasion to be obvious. He failed in his attempt to keep you from getting saved, but if he can convince you to compromise your covenant rights, choose flesh instead of Spirit, and live carnally and not righteously, he can make your witness ineffective.

Be on guard for small opportunities to compromise your faith, no matter how small. Anytime you allow a spiritual compromise—so that you can fit in with others, be accepted, or not offend others—it deposits a tare that will grow and ultimately bear a harvest that is contrary to your destiny as a believer.

Satan is the enemy who plants seed on land he doesn't own. The devil wants to choke out God's Word that is growing inside you. The devil no longer has a right to you. You are now in God's kingdom. You belong to Jesus. The enemy is trying to plant seeds in territory that is off limits to him.

Please understand, most plants don't die overnight but over time. This is what the devil is banking on. If you subject yourself to people, places, and things that are contrary to righteousness, over time the line between what is right and what is wrong begins to blur, and acts of compromise will begin to manifest. These acts can be traced to seed (thoughts) that gained entry into your mind. They are thoughts that your body ultimately acted out.

Beware of doctrine that says, "Everyone is OK; we're all God's children." This is a lie! Only those who have received the saving grace of Jesus Christ are the children of God. The conflict we see raging in society regarding lifestyles, marriage, and the family unit is emblematic of a war of attrition between seed: the seed of Satan and the seed of the woman. The body of Christ is empowered for conquest. We possess authority in Jesus' name to steadily advance, conquering new territory and winning the masses for Christ until His return. This can only happen by faith, and faith comes by hearing (Romans 10:17), in some cases repetitive hearing, until His word resonates inside your spirit.

The devil knows this. He understands that God created you to hear naturally and spiritually. He knows that faith comes by hearing the Word; therefore, he has concluded that unbelief will also come by hearing. The devil's objective is to steal, kill, and destroy (John 10:10). He hates you at a level of hatred that the human mind cannot comprehend. He desperately wants to steal the privileges of your birthright, kill you and your family, and destroy your destiny.

Satan is seeking people he can devour (1 Peter 5:8). To accomplish his plan, he attacks daily from the outside, trying to get inside. He works through your soul via suggestive thoughts to destroy you from within by sowing seeds of doubt and unbelief. However, I want you to know God's plan is infinitely more powerful. Matthew 15:13 says our Father has the power to pull up by the root anything in you that He didn't plant. Jesus has come that you might have life beyond mere existence—a life of abundance (John 10:10).

## You Are God's Plan

Your heavenly Father wants you to be confident in Him. He has a plan for your life. No matter how things appear today, your future is God's history. He's already been where you're going. He created you with purpose in accordance with His will (Ephesians 2:10). He didn't make a mistake when He made you. You are fearfully and wonderfully made (Psalm 139:14)! Everything about you was designed by God to solve a problem on earth. When we read about Jeremiah, we understand that his purpose on earth was predetermined before he was formed in his mother's womb (Jeremiah 1:5). His life on earth was God's idea, and the same is true regarding you! God hasn't changed. You are His plan.

According to Isaiah 46:9, God is God alone, and He proves this by not starting a project without finishing it first. He's not like man. The God who began a good work in you will complete what He began:

> *Being confident of this very thing, that he which hath begun a good work in you will perform it until the day of Jesus Christ.*
> **—Philippians 1:6**

God's plan for your life, your preordained purpose and path, are all a function of your relationship with Him. These are not religion's considerations. Religion puts its focus on what we have to do, while relationship focuses on understanding what we have received. Religion puts the onus on personal performance, but relationship gets its strength through receiving. The only performance that should concern you is that of His promises in your life:

> *There are many devices in a man's heart; nevertheless the counsel of the LORD, that shall stand.*
> **—Proverbs 19:21**

Notice that He didn't leave it up to you to choose your mother or your father. He didn't ask your opinion about the environment you would be raised in. He wasn't reluctant to expose you to a wide range of hardships. I'm sure you can point to things you've experienced in life that seemed unfair and appeared to be in direct conflict with what the Word promises. You may look at others and get this feeling of inadequacy inside you, but I have great news for you: feelings can be misleading. All feelings of inadequacy have satanic origins. You might feel less than, but you possess the greater One inside you (1 John 4:4). There is enough God in you right now to impact the world for Christ. God made you to be a carrier of His presence to reveal Christ to the world. All you've experienced in life was prearranged by God for this time in human history to impact humanity in a unique way— He has called you. God needed a unique channel to work through to bring about change in your generation.

Rejoice! God built into you an overcoming anointing (God's empowerment in flesh). This anointing is designed to continually cause you to triumph through every adverse circumstance you will ever face in your lifetime. God puts His guarantee on you with the following verse:

*There hath no temptation taken you but such as is common to man: but God is faithful, who will not suffer you to be tempted above that ye are able; but will with the temptation also make a way to escape, that ye may be able to bear it.*
**—1 Corinthians 10:13**

The aforementioned verse makes it clear that there is no temptation any believer will ever face that he or she cannot come through triumphantly. God made you a winner before you were conceived. Let that sink in. Greatness was in you before you started. As a matter of fact, God made you a success in life and bragged about it at the announcement of your birth.

You are strategically positioned to perform exploits for your King and His kingdom. There is no one like you in the past, present, or future.

## *You Have a Responsibility*

With this uniqueness comes responsibility. You are responsible to never compare yourself to anyone else. Comparing yourself, your assignment, or your gifting to anyone else is a form of covetousness.

Let me elaborate for a moment. God made man one time. He didn't need to remake man after Adam's transgression. Did you catch that? Even after Adam sinned, the uniqueness of Adam was so pervasive and so far reaching that God didn't have to start over again. God just unveiled the next step in His eternal plan of redemption. Adam was a masterpiece, robust, and durable. There was no need to make a copy.

Adam had a unique assignment, and so do you. Stop trying to be someone you're not. You will only be second-rate by trying to be someone else. You can learn from another, but you can never be another. Many believers lose their identities trying to be someone or something they were never created to be.

There is only one Mona Lisa painting. It's in the Louvre in Paris. If I saw it someplace else, I would know it's an imitation of the original. You are the best at being you. To try to be like someone else would make you a second-rate someone else. God doesn't deal with second-rate. Learn from others, but don't compare yourself to others or try to become them. Your story is uniquely yours.

CHAPTER TWO

# Following Jesus

Why have things played out the way they have? Why has life been such a struggle? Why did you lose your job? Why didn't you get accepted into the school you were believing God for? Why is your marriage such a struggle at times? Why does it seem like things aren't getting any better? Why does your plight seem little different than that of an unbeliever? These are all fair questions.

## *The Only Way*

Let's start this discussion by understanding our relationship to God. People are the single most important thing to God. God unconditionally loves every person who has ever been born. Despite the lies of Satan, God is not mad at you. He's not even mad at sinners. Where sin once dominated mankind, now the grace of God is infinitely superior and present to save all who put their faith and confidence in Christ. The Bible makes it clear that the only way to God is through Jesus (John 14:6). Jesus is the only door.

Let me explain my point, in case you're reading this book and you have a different belief.

Suppose there was a house you desperately wanted to enter, and there was only one door that granted you entry, but that door was locked with a combination lock. How can you enter unless you know the right combination of right, left, and right turns, along with the correct series of numbers to unlock the door? No matter how strong you are, you can't break the lock. Human strength and effort will never suffice. You can talk to the lock, but it has no regard for reasoning. You can try a key, but the lock won't relate to a key. There is only one way to unlock the door. You must obey the instructions of the one who possesses the house.

Mankind is incapable of knowing the route to get to God apart from Jesus. No matter how intelligent, educated, or privileged we are, we cannot know God or have a relationship with Him without Jesus.

Jesus is the only way: "Jesus saith unto him, I am the way, the truth, and the life: no man cometh unto the Father, but by me" (John 14:6).

*There is a way that seemeth right unto a man, but the end thereof are the ways of death.*
**—Proverbs 16:25**

People struggle when told that Jesus is the only way, and the reason is simple: when the route is unknown, something has to fill the void. There are no empty spaces in the earth—something will always fill the void. Darkness will reign where there is an absence of light. Where there is a void of knowledge, something called ignorance will fill the space. So, when people don't know the way, they will inevitably create their own way.

## *Man's Alternative*

I believe the Bible makes it clear that religion is Satan's alternative to relationship with God. Relationship centers its focus on love for God and His way of being right. Religion gets its strength in adherence to a love for dos and don'ts that can never appease God:

> *For you were included in the death of Christ and have died with him to the religious system and powers of this world. Don't retreat back to being bullied by the standards and opinions of religion—for example, their strict requirements, "You can't associate with that person!" or, "Don't eat that!" or, "You can't touch that!" These are the doctrines of men and corrupt customs that are worthless to help you spiritually.*
> **—Colossians 2:20–22** *(TPT)*

The religious system of Jesus' day directly opposed the teachings of Jesus. The representatives of the Pharisee and the Sadducee went so far as to accuse Jesus of casting out the devil using the devil's power (Mark 3:22).

Religion seems good, looks good, and appears good, but it leads to destruction.

Recall the etymology of the word *religion*, which comes from the Latin *religio*, meaning "obligation, bond, reverence," or perhaps based on the Latin *religare*, meaning "to bind."[4]

Religion binds or imprisons people from the freedom of a loving relationship with God. Jesus is the only way to that loving relationship with the Father. There is no other name given under heaven whereby men must be saved. Religion says the devil is your greatest adversary. The Bible says something different; it says ignorance is your greatest opponent. That's why I wrote this book—to rid you of ignorance of who you are in Christ, the kingdom you possess, and His purpose for your life.

I'm convinced any person who rejects Jesus accepts religion by default. Religion comes in many forms: Baha'i, Buddhism, Christianity, Confucianism, Hinduism, Islam, Jainism, Judaism, Shinto, Sikhism, Taoism, and Zoroastrianism. Add atheism, scientism, mysticism, and Gnosticism. They are all religions. And they all—including the religion of Christianity—focus on performance. None of them—including the religion of Christianity—focus on relationship.

Following Jesus is about following Jesus. It isn't about following a list of dos and don'ts.

Am I a believer in Jesus? Absolutely. Am I a Christian in the sense of religion? No.

Recall that the early believers did not call themselves Christians—they called themselves disciples of the Lord. *Christian* is what the pagans termed them when they saw that the early believers in Antioch followed a man called Christ (Acts 11:26; Acts 9:1–2).

The Bible is not a religious book. Simply stated, the Bible is a law book that reveals a King, His kingdom, and His children. Jesus was the way the Father chose to reestablish His kingdom, His life, and His nature back into humanity—all of which takes place inside every born-again believer, *not* in someone who is religious.

This is why, if you study the ministry of Jesus, you discover that His true opponents were the religious Pharisees, Sadducees, and scribes. The religious people demanded Jesus' crucifixion. Even Pilate was prepared to release Jesus, but the religious leaders threatened to petition Caesar about Pilot's leniency. At that point, Pilate acquiesced to their demand to crucify Him (Matthew 27:21–24).

## *But God!*

Jesus—your maker, the author and finisher of your faith (Hebrews 12:2)—determined before the world existed to take your uniqueness, your experiences good and bad, and fashion you in such a way to appeal to specific subsets of people who lie in darkness. He did all this before you were born!

Pay close attention as you read the following scriptures about a young teenager named Gideon:

> *And the angel of the LORD appeared unto him, and said unto him, The LORD is with thee, thou mighty man of valour.*
>
> *And Gideon said unto him, Oh my Lord, if the LORD be with us, why then is all this befallen us? and where be all his miracles which our fathers told us of, saying, Did not the LORD bring us up from Egypt? but now the LORD hath forsaken us, and delivered us into the hands of the Midianites.*
>
> *And the LORD looked upon him, and said, Go in this thy might, and thou shalt save Israel from the hand of the Midianites: have not I sent thee?*
>
> *And he said unto him, Oh my Lord, wherewith shall I save Israel? behold, my family is poor in Manasseh, and I am the least in my father's house.*
>
> *And the LORD said unto him, surely I will be with thee, and thou shalt smite the Midianites as one man.*
> *—Judges 6:12–16*

Because of their sin, Israel was being continually raided by multiple foreign nations. Their goal was to destroy the land and its people. To solve Israel's problem, God pre-prepared a champion named Gideon. Before Gideon was conceived, God had already fully preordained

Israel's solution in the form of a poor, uneducated, disregarded, undervalued, and unaffirmed young man born on the wrong side of the tracks to the poorest family in Israel.

God doesn't need much to work with! He's God. On the outside, Gideon was the least qualified for the assignment, but God judges the inside.

Aren't you glad God doesn't judge you the way people do? Gideon was disqualified based on his circumstances—*but God*. You need to practice telling yourself, *but God*.

Gideon is so convinced of his inadequacies he debates with his maker about his qualifications.

Who knows better about a product—the customer or the manufacturer? Who knows what you're truly capable of—you or your maker? Look at your circumstances and say to them: *but God!* When you release your faith to say that something from inside you will confront something outside of you, you step into the realm of the supernatural, where all things are possible. You cannot be what you refuse to be, and you cannot go where you refuse to go.

What God wants to do through your life will infinitely exceed your expectations. God doesn't need your ability; He simply needs your availability. A "yes" to God will take you further in life than a Harvard degree.

Please understand, He doesn't need to consult with your circumstances to validate your potential. You are His idea. He built His potential inside you before you were born. Every human being born onto this planet is born with a Jesus mandate. That's why every human is looking for God—some choose Islam, some choose Buddhism, some choose Hinduism, but everybody is hardwired by God to submit to a being greater than themselves.

This is why it is vital that you recognize who you are in Christ. The power of God that dwells on the inside of you is demanding a release. There are rivers of living water ready to flow out of your spirit, words ready to be unleashed, supernatural works ready to be manifested. Your circumstances have no bearing on the supernatural potential that resides in you.

## *Hardwired for Victory*

Without an understanding of your supernatural potential, you run the risk of low spiritual esteem—the same disease Gideon suffered from until he said yes to God:

> *And the LORD looked upon him, and said, Go in this thy might, and thou shalt save Israel from the hand of the Midianites: have not I sent thee?*
>
> *And he said unto him, Oh my Lord, wherewith shall I save Israel? behold, my family is poor in Manasseh, and I am the least in my father's house.*
>
> *—Judges 6:14–15*

Remind yourself daily that you can do anything God says you can do. There is no condemnation in the kingdom you represent. You have no need to feel sorry for yourself.

The Bible is a law book. When you understand how the laws operate, you unlock God's ability to appropriate His precious promises. The great news is that not one of His promises has ever failed—not one (Joshua 23:14). What God says about you is your reality. Think about it: Doesn't the manufacturer inform the customer in writing (i.e., in the product manual) what the product is capable of doing? The manual tells you the dos and don'ts and where to go for repairs. Your confidence is in God, the One who designed, produced, and affirmed you:

> *For we are his workmanship, created in Christ Jesus unto*

*good works, which God hath before ordained that we should walk in them.*
**—Ephesians 2:10**

There are certain biblical principles that fuel my endurance. They keep me going when I feel like giving up. I believe the next statement will do the same for you. When you discover your purpose and start moving toward it, God unlocks every spiritual blessing locked inside you, so you leave your mark on humanity:

*Blessed be the God and Father of our Lord Jesus Christ, who hath blessed us with all spiritual blessings in heavenly places in Christ: According as he hath chosen us in him before the foundation of the world, that we should be holy and without blame before him in love.*
**—Ephesians 1:3-4**

You were chosen in advance of your trouble. The wherewithal to overcome every problem, trouble, and bad circumstance has been pre-deposited in your spirit.

The power of activation for victory is tied to your response to adversity. In my teaching at Kingdom Living Church, I instruct to be careful of first reactions to problems. The devil is not spiritual, and he has no idea what's working or not working until you react. To help ensure you react incorrectly, Satan presents the spirit of fear. To help the believer react correctly: "For God hath not given us the spirit of fear; but of power, and of love, and of a sound mind" (2 Timothy 1:7).

Furthermore, we possess the spirit of faith: "We having the same spirit of faith, according as it is written, I believed, and therefore have I spoken; we also believe, and therefore speak" (2 Corinthians 4:13).

In any case, and in every circumstance, you're going to

have to say something. Death and life are in the power of your tongue (Proverbs 18:21). You get to determine the fruit it produces.

Remember, you were hardwired for victory before your deployment on earth. How it looks is irrelevant. The determining factor is how you think. Thank God for the testimonies of others, but you need your own testimonies. Always remember, past triumphs play into future victories. Learn from David:

> *Thy servant slew both the lion and the bear: and this uncircumcised Philistine shall be as one of them, seeing he hath defied the armies of the living God.*
>
> *David said moreover, The LORD that delivered me out of the paw of the lion, and out of the paw of the bear, he will deliver me out of the hand of this Philistine. And Saul said unto David, Go, and the LORD be with thee.*
> **—1 Samuel 17:36–37**

David made it clear that the source of his confidence was God! He said the Lord delivered him out of the paw of the bear. But if you think about it, we only know about David's exploits because he was willing to take on a lion and a bear. David was courageous. David was willing to confront a lion that stole from his father.

Confidence can help you conquer the unimaginable. We would never know that a one-term senator from Chicago could become president (Barack Obama) or that a businessman with no political experience (Donald Trump) could become the leader of the free world. Regardless of one's political leanings, we should applaud their courage to step into the political ring and compete. You have to be willing to take on the champ to be the champ.

God wants you to be confident in the face of adversity.

A right relationship with God breeds confidence. Confidence in God translates into confidence in your inner man. He doesn't want you to count yourself out at the thought of a battle. Always remember, "to the victor belong the spoils."[5]

I'm not saying to put confidence in your flesh! We are forbidden to do so (Philippians 3:2–7). But you need to know that according to God, you're worth it. You have extreme value to God. Whatever God does on the earth, He does in cooperation with a human. That person is you. Therefore, you should possess some self-worth. As I mentioned before, you were hardwired for victory before the foundations of the earth, so walk confidently with that in mind.

CHAPTER THREE

# Only One of You

I heard a wise man once say, half the battle is just showing up.

Think about Joshua. What did the Lord say to Joshua when He anointed him to follow in the footsteps of Moses? Be strong. Do not fear. Be of good courage (Joshua 1:6–9, paraphrased). First, I want you to see where promotion comes from. All promotion comes from God. When God says it's your time, it's your time. He does everything in divine order. God always determines timing.

It was not until Moses was dead that Joshua received his elevation. Joshua didn't pressure Moses to get his opportunity. Joshua was consumed with his assignment to serve. When you give yourself away to serve in another man's purpose, you allow God to prepare you for something great. This is true in my own life. My wife and I served Bishop Andrew and Pastor Viveca Merritt of Straight Gate International Church for over twenty years. We weren't cognizant of it at the time, but we were being prepared for an assignment tailor-made for us in Grand Blanc, Michigan.

God reveals Himself in the Bible as a husbandman

(John 15:1). The word *husbandman* is defined in *Merriam-Webster Dictionary* as "one who plows and cultivates land: [a] farmer; a specialist in a branch of farm."[6] It was God's decision to plant us in Grand Blanc, our wealthy place. He skillfully used our spiritual upbringing and twenty years of service at Straight Gate International Church to prepare my family and me to minister before Him, serving mankind through His anointing.

I want you to see clearly in Joshua chapter 1 that God didn't ask Joshua for his opinion. He clarified the mission, assured Joshua of His abiding presence, gave him a clear target to judge by, and informed him of the power within him to dominate any opponent he might face. However, the determining factor of success or failure depended on Joshua's courage, endurance, and what he gave focus to. Joshua already had courage and strength within him. God merely said Joshua had to make up his mind to *be* it.

Did you catch that? God didn't have to make Joshua strong and courageous; he already was. God had already put these qualities in Joshua. But Joshua had to make the decision to be what God preordained him to be. To be something is a choice. Make the choice today to be what God called you to be so you can do what He ordained you to do before the world was created.

## *Set Your Focus*

Joshua 1 also reveals to us that Joshua's potential was to be derived from his focus. God gave Joshua the secret to maximize his potential. He directed Joshua's focus. Please understand, your capacity to be is derived directly and indirectly from your focus. You will gravitate to what you focus on—and you will ultimately become what you gravitate toward.

Let me explain the power of focus in simplistic terms.

A laser is nothing but highly focused light. Without focus, a light will illuminate a room. But if you focus a light to an extreme, you unlock its potential to cut through steel. The Bible reveals this truth. Focus is so powerful, it even moves God to act. Do you recall the story of the Tower of Babel in Genesis 11? The whole earth—all of humanity—came together and decided to build a tower up to the heavens, to make a name for themselves (Genesis 11:4). They made so much progress that the Lord concluded, "Behold, the people is one, and they have all one language; and this they begin to do: and now nothing will be restrained from them, which they have imagined to do" (Genesis 11:6).

Did you see that? "Behold, the people is one." Though their intentions were unrighteous, they tapped into the same principle as God. A unifying focus, agreement, and unity make anything possible.

Consider also what is arguably the most important verse in the Torah to any Jewish person. It speaks to the harmony and focus of the Father, Son, and Holy Spirit: "Hear, O Israel: The LORD our God is one LORD" (Deuteronomy 6:4).

Focus is an attribute of oneness. Oneness originates from God. Oneness makes any endeavor feasible. This principal works in business, in church, in families, in marriage, and in individuals. We see examples of believers as well as unbelievers putting the power of oneness to work for their respective goals.

## *Your Oneness*

Let me go on a tangent regarding oneness for a moment. The Word of God can speak for itself:

*For there are three that bear record in heaven, the Father, the Word, and the Holy Ghost: and these three are one.*

*And there are three that bear witness in earth, the Spirit, and the water, and the blood: and these three agree in one.*
*—1 John 5:7-8*

*There is neither Jew nor Greek, there is neither bond nor free, there is neither male nor female: for ye are all one in Christ Jesus.*
*—Galatians 3:28*

With the aforementioned scriptures in mind, it shouldn't surprise you that He only made *one* of you to change the world. He only needs *one* of you!

Your oneness makes you incomparable. No one who has ever lived is exactly like you. No one has your voice tone, your fingerprint, your DNA, or your personality. God made you a singular masterpiece. This understanding prohibits you from comparing yourself to anyone or anything else that has been created:

*I will cry unto God most high; unto God that performeth all things for me.*
*—Psalm 57:2*

He chose your mother and your father. Don't get caught up on how you got here or the environment you were born into. God knows exactly what He's doing. Your success has already been determined before you were deployed. I use the word *deployed* because it accurately depicts how intentional God is. You were born with an assignment that the world cannot do without. The notion that you're some lowly worm is unscriptural and demonic. David said:

*When I consider thy heavens, the work of thy fingers, the moon and the stars, which thou hast ordained; What is man, that thou art mindful of him? and the son of man, that thou visitest him? For thou hast made him a little lower than the angels, and hast crowned him with glory and honour.*

*—Psalm 8:3-5*

The word *angels* in verse 5 in the original text is *Elohim*, not angels.[7] In fact, the American Standard Version translates this verse as, "For thou hast made him [man] but little lower than God [Hebrew *Elohim*]"(ASV). Wow! That's a huge difference. Man was made to rule the earth and transform it to resemble heaven.

## *Release Your Faith*

God doesn't need numbers. He needs faith:

*And Jonathan said to the young man that bare his armour, Come, and let us go over unto the garrison of these uncircumcised: it may be that the LORD will work for us: for there is no restraint to the LORD to save by many or by few.*

*—1 Samuel 14:6*

My recommendation is to let God be God, and hang in there long enough to see the conclusion of the entire matter. Keep a steady pace. When Moses stopped at the Red Sea and began to consider his circumstances, God told him to get up and move forward:

*And the LORD said unto Moses, Wherefore criest thou unto me? speak unto the children of Israel, that they go forward.*

*—Exodus 14:15*

This notion that you lack purpose and that your current circumstances define you is a lie. Don't confuse where you are with where you're going. Don't get frustrated because your beginning is small. Jesus is committed to make your later days better than your former. I want you to *Selah*—which means pause and reflect—for a moment regarding your destiny. Release your faith right now, knowing that God is causing everything to work together for your good.

CHAPTER FOUR

# Personal Stewardship

No leader worth their salt has had an easy road. Every pastor I regard has scars. I have deep scars from my pursuit of God. But how we steward our circumstances determines our outcomes. We steward well when we allow God's presence to sustain us in the midst of trials.

Joseph was a man who stewarded well what he was given. He allowed God to infiltrate every situation, which caused all of his endeavors to flourish. Genesis 37 tells us Joseph's brothers' jealousy intensified when they realized their father loved him more than all his other sons. Joseph's pronouncement of his dream that he was destined to be a ruler over them only intensified their hatred for their brother. They sold him into slavery, and the odds were stacked against him.

From the outside, Joseph was a convicted felon with a death sentence on his life. However, I want you to see the distinguishing factor in Joseph's life: "And the patriarchs, moved with envy, sold Joseph into Egypt: *but God was with him*" (Acts 7:9, emphasis added).

God's presence in your situation, not the size of your opponent, is the deciding factor. Your awareness of God's active presence will breed confidence in your heart no matter the odds against you. Remember, God is your judge and law-giver. He is the only One who determines who wins or loses (James 4:12). As Bishop Merritt would often say, "It's His manifested presence that makes the difference."

## *Effective Stewardship*

Jesus—who is Lord over the church—will never give you what you cannot manage. That goes for membership, money, positions, houses, jobs, and so forth. Let me say that again: God will never give you what you cannot effectively manage, make grow, flourish, thrive, and produce fruit.

All these gimmicks advertising for you to "grow your church in five easy steps" and "do this to see rapid church growth" are perplexing to me. When I read my Bible, I see clearly that Jesus grows His church. Steward what He gives you and allow Him to permeate every aspect of it—and even in the hardest times, growth will come.

God values stewardship above all other earthly exploits. This point is evident in creation.

God gave Adam an unfinished earth. Adam was empowered with dominion to finish the work, spreading the garden over the entire earth (Genesis 1:28). The garden represented the presence of God. Adam's job was to spread the presence of God over every inch of this planet. God made the heavens, the earth, and planted a garden eastward in Eden. God then goes on record to say He could not proceed without an ordained manager for His creation. Reflect on the following passage:

*And every plant of the field before it was in the earth, and every herb of the field before it grew: for the LORD God had not caused it to rain upon the earth, and there was not a man to till the ground.*

—*Genesis 2:5*

I want you to think about that last clause. There was no man to dominate the earth. Therefore, God would not cause it to rain. Without a man, the rain would cause things to grow without order. As I previously stated, your God is a God of order. When He gives you something, He expects you to finish it. God never gives you anything to do that's already finished. He requires you to use your faith to cause that thing to be on earth as it is in heaven.

We find this management principle in the New Testament as well, in a parable Jesus shared about the master who distributed talents to his stewards:

> *And unto one he gave five talents, to another two, and to another one; to every man according to his several ability; and straightway took his journey.*
>
> —*Matthew 25:15*

The Lord gives out the quantity of talents to each man *in accordance to his capacity to manage them*. Notice he didn't give all individuals the same number of talents. This is a vital key in the kingdom of God. Management is everything to God. To whom much is given, much is required in the way of stewardship (Luke 12:48).

Thank God for what He has given you. Activate your faith by speaking His Word and utilize the resource of hard work to produce disciples for Christ, whether a few people or many thousands. Learn the lessons of managing where you are today.

I thank God for the leaders of large churches as well as small churches. I'm convinced a small congregation is not proof that a pastor or leadership lacks faith or vision. After all, God can choose the smallest group of people to be an example of His love and devotion. The Israelites were a small nation, remember: "The LORD did not set his love upon you, nor choose you, because ye were more in number than any people; for ye were the fewest of all people." (Deuteronomy 7:7).

Whether our resources are few or many, what we do with what we already possess is vitally important. The Lord assesses how well we manage our resources.

In the parable of the talents in Matthew 25, the steward who was most productive and exhibited the best oversight was given more. The servant who did nothing with what he had been given lost his stewardship role. What he had was given to the most productive servant. When Jesus fed the five thousand, He instructed his disciples to "gather up the fragments that remain, that nothing be lost" (John 6:12). God esteems productivity and despises waste. He is the greatest economist of all time. He also expects a return of His investment in you.

## *Right Now*

Your heavenly Father is slow to anger and gracious in every way (Psalm 103:8). When you begin to understand the intensity of His love for you, you won't give up on yourself. More importantly, you'll resist the urge to give up on others.

As a leader in the body of Christ, I've made mistakes; I've missed God; I have regrets. But God considered all my sins and miscalculations when He called my name. The same is true for you. He knew there would be times when you would falter, but He still sent Jesus to die for your sins. As you read this book, let the Holy Spirit minister to you to receive a new beginning from Him.

There's an anointing in Jesus that's designed to jump start your assignment. Whether the joy of your salvation has waned or your life shows no signs of progress, I want you to know that Jesus is a quickening Spirit. His very life and nature is in you right now to turn everything around. Be confident of this very thing—the same power that raised Jesus from the dead is present and ready to turn your life around right now. That's the part I like—right now. Be it unto you according to your faith—right now. Believe that angels are being dispatched on your behalf—right now. I believe it's your time for manifestation of long-awaited promises—right now. During His earthly ministry, Jesus spoke of heaven's reality on earth. In doing so, He unleashed a supernatural reality on earth. And He invites us to do even greater works than He did:

> *Verily, verily, I say unto you, He that believeth on me, the works that I do shall he do also; and greater works than these shall he do; because I go unto my Father.*
> *—John 14:12*

Remember, relationship is everything to God. Proverbs 24:16 states: "For a just man falleth seven times, and riseth up again: but the wicked shall fall into mischief." If you have sinned, repent and move forward. Receive His forgiveness and keep moving forward in Christ.

CHAPTER FIVE

# The Master Plan

If you take anything away from this book, I pray you embrace the following statement.

*You are central to God's master plan of restoration.*

God chose you just like He chose Abraham, Moses, and David. Any notion that you are insignificant and unimportant to God is a satanic concept. And while we celebrate the accomplishments of these great men, they can't compare to you.

So just in case you're currently encountering feelings of insignificance, they're temporary. You have extreme value to God. Your birth is proof of your importance to God. The fulfillment of your purpose is a subplot to His overall plan to restore the kingdom of God back to mankind.

## *Restore the Kingdom*

Jesus came to the earth to restore the kingdom and authority Adam lost when he sinned in Eden. You have been empowered by the Holy Spirit to enforce the mandate of the kingdom. You have been equipped with the name of Jesus to outlast your latest test.

The fact you have a flesh body confirms you have authority on earth. Only beings with a flesh and blood body have rightful authority on earth. This is why the Holy Spirit dwells inside of you. He cannot legally dwell on earth without the appropriate temple. Your body is the dwelling place of the most-high God (1 Corinthians 6:19).

The devil doesn't have an earthly body. That makes his presence on earth illegal. Demons are here illegally. They don't have a body. Where is the devil's mother? To have a body, a spirit has to be birthed through a woman. A spirit comes through the birth canal of a woman. Now you can better understand why the devil chose to approach Eve in the garden and not Adam. He understood the necessity of birth through a woman for legality.

The devil wasn't born! He is illegal. He has no right to anything on earth. He has no right to you, your family, your possessions, or your destiny. What he now possesses, he gained through deception and mankind's ignorance of God's Word.

This is why evil spirits work hard to possess human bodies to give them legal precedence. The Scriptures reveal it's hard for demons to take possession of human bodies.

When you look at Matthew chapter 8, you see that human real estate is so hard to come by that an entire legion of demons crammed into one man. Roughly six thousand demons dwelled in one man who wasn't saved, and yet they didn't have the power to kill him. Six thousand demons couldn't kill one unsaved man! When Jesus cast the demons out, notice that they prayed to Jesus to let them go into the pigs. Yes, demons pray to Jesus too!

Only spirits with flesh bodies have a right to exercise authority on earth.

Now you know why Jesus had to be born of a virgin. He needed legal authority on earth. This is signified by his possession of an earthly body. The body He possessed was named Jesus, but the Spirit in the body was called Christ.

Praise God! You possess the same authority Jesus possessed in His earthly ministry. How is that possible? Because you possess the same power supply He possessed—the Holy Spirit.

That's who Adam lost when he revolted against God in the garden. The spirit of rebellion that Lucifer unleashed on earth and in the atmosphere is the same spirit of rebellion that Adam expressed when he ate of the fruit reserved for God.

Adam lost it. Jesus restored it. What is *it*? The kingdom of God.

Adam lost Him. The Father promised Him. Jesus sent Him. Who? The Holy Spirit, who is God on earth, living inside temples not made with hands.

The Holy Spirit's mission is to cause Christ to be perfectly formed in you. He gently leads and guides, instructs and corrects. He appointed the five-fold ministry for the perfecting of the saints.

Jesus came from heaven to the earth to restore the kingdom of heaven back to the human family.

## The Message

Highlight this statement, put a star by it, and meditate on it: *Jesus came to earth to preach and teach one singular message—the message of the kingdom of heaven.* For me, this is one of the most important truths that I have discovered in God's Word.

This statement brings a basic clarity to the overall plan of God for His people and their rulership over the earth. Look at a sample of major biblical characters who spoke, repeatedly and passionately, of the kingdom of heaven as their overarching theme:

- John the Baptist (Matthew 3)

- Jesus (Mark 1, Matthew 4, Matthew 10, Matthew 11, Acts 1, Matthew 13, Matthew 18, Matthew 20, Matthew 22, Matthew 25, Mark 4)

- The disciples (Matthew 10; Acts 8)

- The apostle Paul (Acts 28)

From the fall of man onward, everything in God's plan and timing hinged on the reintroduction of the kingdom lost.

If you're wondering how this is relevant to you in the midst of money problems, health problems, relationship issues, and daily life—it affects everything.

The kingdom is the government of heaven. The kingdom is heaven's system of the rule of law. It's what gave Adam the authority and methodology to rule the animals, fish, insects, birds, and plants.

Without the kingdom, Adam and his descendants were forced to create an alternative system. A system infinitely inferior and relegated to eventually collapse under its own weight.

Every man-made form of government the world has ever conceived has ultimately failed. Communism, socialism, dictatorships, totalitarianism, Marxism, and so forth have all failed with time—and the same will be true with democracy. As great as the Roman Empire was, it ultimately imploded due to its inherent unrighteousness, corruption, and greed. The great Grecian Empire was destroyed, and Greece today is economically in shambles and has never recovered.

The only government that cannot be destroyed is the government of heaven, what the Bible calls the kingdom of heaven. And if you are born again, that kingdom is inside you right now, ready to transform you and everything around you. The kingdom possesses all the power you will ever need to fulfill your destiny on earth.

## *Fulfill Your Purpose*

Everyone experiences bumps along the way, and maybe you have a few scars as proof things have been a struggle at times. You're still standing though, so start giving God praise. You're still here! That's proof God has more of His goodness in store for you. Feel good about your future because He has declared that the end of a thing is better than its beginning (Ecclesiastes 7:8).

So, maybe you have to start all over again. Maybe things didn't go as planned, you don't have much, and your beginning is small.

I want to encourage you. You're reading this book as a result of your hunger and thirst for the kingdom of God and His righteousness. Righteousness is God's way of being right. You can't hunger for Him without Him satisfying your appetite. Like the woman at the well, He is prepared to give you water that will satisfy your thirst for a lifetime (John 4:6–14). Isaiah 44:3 says, "For I will pour water upon him that is thirsty, and floods upon the dry ground."

I'm confident God is preparing to move in your life in such a way that a nonbeliever will acknowledge it was God. Settle in your heart that God is using people, places, and things to position you for fulfillment of your purpose in accordance with His will. He's already supplied you with every spiritual blessing you will ever need for a lifetime, in heavenly places, out of the reach of Satan. Now as you walk by faith, showing your reliance upon Jesus, He activates the treasure hidden inside you to make your mark on the world for Christ.

There is no part of you that His power cannot transform. There is no situation too bad, no hole too deep, no body too sick that the power of God cannot address. Believe God today! Make Him your only source for everything. Remember your heavenly Father owns everything (Psalm 24:1). He is Lord of the whole earth.

## *God Is Your Source*

Years ago, I was an account executive for an automotive company in Michigan. I had been a good employee for roughly six years. I was ready for a change, and God opened a door to a position of a lifetime that could lead to me becoming CEO of a $16 million automotive supply company. I accepted the offer at the other company.

The day I planned to submit my letter of resignation, I was scheduled to have lunch with the owner of my new employer. We had negotiated for him to give me a signing bonus of $25,000, and I was going to receive the check during lunch. I was so excited.

The day I was scheduled to meet with my new boss for lunch, my current boss wanted to meet with me in her office. When I arrived, a human resources person was in the room, too. She told me they appreciated my work, but the decision had been made to let me go. I was stunned and saddened, even though I was preparing to give her my letter of resignation that day. Her eyes teared up and so did mine. I truly appreciated the people I worked for, and they appreciated me.

As she concluded the meeting, she said, "We don't normally do this, but we're giving you a check for $25,000 for your work and service to the company. This decision came from the owner."

Well, my tears started drying up! I left company A with a $25,000 check and went to lunch an hour later and received another check for $25,000 from company B.

Remember: God is always the source, and people are

His resources. Don't ever get these two transposed. People are never your source. That position is reserved for God alone. Your job doesn't have the capacity to take care of you. Your supply is authored in heaven. God can use any resource on earth to further your progress on earth because He owns everything. Recall how God commanded a widow woman to sustain the prophet Elijah (1 Kings 17).

When did God lead Elijah to the widow? After first leading him to a brook that dried up! Day by day it seemed like Elijah's resource was getting smaller and smaller. What do you do when it looks like the resource you thought would never end dries up? Do you take matters into your own hands? Do you go back to where you came from and seek out old acquaintances?

We should do what Elijah did: wait until the Lord gives us the word to move. We can gain kingdom insight by looking at Elijah's story carefully: Elijah didn't move until he heard from the Lord. This reveals Elijah believed God was his only source. His confidence in God not only to lead him, but also to sustain him, produced a dependency upon God's voice.

## *No Matter What*

The voice of God is irresistible to your spirit. However, you must train your soul to yield to your spirit. Your spirit is where the Holy Spirit resides. He dwells in you for the purpose of forming Christ in you. This is why you can never give up. There is no provision for retreat or surrender in our covenant of grace. The Holy Spirit works continuously perfecting the things which concern you. He has the power to take every mistake and work it together for your good and the good of others. The Bible says it this way: "…Christ in you, the hope of glory" (Colossians 1:27).

The resurrection power of Christ now dwells in you, ready to cause havoc in Satan's kingdom as rivers of living water flow out of you (John 7:38). With this in mind, what do you do when you don't know what to do? What biblical insight do you adhere to in times of crisis? The remedy is to follow God no matter what. Do what the Word says no matter what. Trust Him and lean not on your own understanding, experience, and education. Where God is taking you is new. You may not have a point of reference to draw from. That's not a weakness but a strength and shows His love for you. God will put you in situations where you are completely reliant upon Him. He will always affirm His status as your only source in your life.

God doesn't run a co-op system where He shares the responsibility of taking care of you with someone or something else. Your dependence on Him attracts Him. Your obedience motivates Him. Your words of faith move Him.

Recall Abraham, who believed God despite how his circumstances looked—who believed he would be the father of nations even though he was old and childless. God credited Abraham's unrelenting trust in God's promise as righteousness. (Romans 4:17–22).

So, we see God Himself calling things that be not as though they already existed, and Abraham believing God despite the impossibility of his circumstances.

God will give you something to do that you can't do without His assistance. Abraham believed, in old age, that his body could produce seed that would result in many nations. God was clearly impressed and declared Abraham righteous. Righteousness is the chief attribute of God's kingdom.

Romans 14:17 says that "the kingdom of God is not meat and drink; but righteousness, and peace, and joy in the Holy Ghost." The order of the kingdom attributes here is significant. Righteousness is first. Hence, "seek ye first the kingdom of God, and his righteousness; and all these things [everything you need] shall be added unto you" (Matthew 6:33).

God spoke Abraham's reality in heaven on earth. Did you catch that? God speaks into your reality on earth as it is in heaven. He doesn't consider your current living conditions. There is not a single trace of impossibility in God's reality of you. You can trust the words God speaks over your life—they will come to pass.

CHAPTER SIX

# Exploits Are Needed

My prayer for you is that God's will be done in your life. His will is the manifestation of the kingdom within you to impact the world and, in doing so, to bring glory to Himself.

Now, the kingdom has to come in order for His will to be done. The kingdom of God is the government of God. The government of God is the ruling authority of God. That ruling authority is inside every born-again believer. When properly expressed through faith, it will demonstrate dominion authority.

## *Dominion Authority*

In layman terms, you will begin to rule and take over. You'll stand out from your peers. Promotion will be commonplace. People who like you as well as those who don't will bless you. God will move on the hearts of people to show you favor.

By favor, I mean shortcuts. Favor removes out of your way the policies, procedures, and restrictions that unsaved and carnal Christians have to abide by. Not so for the person who walks in God's favor. Favor makes life more efficient.

This is just a small sampling of what dominion authority will produce in whosoever believes God. This explains why God emphatically declares it is His good pleasure to give you the kingdom. In doing so, He is legislating His will to be executed in your life day by day, so He can increase you little by little until you overflow. His Word in you is designed to replicate your status in heaven. You are seated in Christ in heavenly places (Ephesians 2:6).

You're not sick in heaven; therefore, His Word declares you're already healed on earth. You're not poor in heaven, so His Word says He will supply all your needs on earth according to His riches in heaven. You're never alone in heaven, thus He declares He will never leave you nor forsake you on earth (Hebrews 13:5).

My point is that His rhema word to you is empowered to make your life like it currently is now in heaven. *Rhema* is the voice of the Holy Spirit speaking to you at the present moment. So when I use the word *rhema*, I mean the Holy Spirit literally speaking a word to you.

When you read your Bible, you are reading the *logos* word, which is the written Word of God. But when He speaks the written Word to you directly, the logos word becomes a rhema word to you.[8] When it's a rhema word, nobody can convince you that God didn't speak to you. A rhema word to you can withstand the passage of time. Twenty years from now, you will be just as convinced as you were when God first spoke it.

One rhema word from God can change your life, your family, and your destiny. There is unlimited power in every word of Scripture. Jesus said one word to Peter, "Come" (Matthew 14:29), and he defied the laws of physics and walked on water. This miracle was so amazing, the Holy Spirit recorded it in Scripture and we're still talking about it two-thousand years later.

That's the power of the lively hope that is within you. The kingdom within you is a power kingdom. It unleashes the power to put you on top. Whatever industry or field of expertise, the kingdom within you will empower you to rule.

The ruling authority of God demonstrates the power of God. The power of God influences the affairs of mankind, but it is only through the demonstration of God's power working through your life that the world will take note. Without power, the world is uninterested. Power is a proof. To be more specific, power is a proof of God's presence in your life.

The presence of His power in your life makes exploits mandatory. Power attracts. The word *exploit* can be simply defined as "a bold or daring feat."[9] Someone somewhere needs to see what's possible. Somebody has to see some form of transformative power in your life in order to be attracted to your heavenly Father.

Without power, there is no way to confirm that your God is the answer to their problem. Power confirms He's in you and that He's the one they've been looking for. I believe God has set aside a segment of society that He has preprogrammed to feed off your testimony. Therefore, don't fear the test. It's the precursor to the testimony. The test is the platform to demonstrate Christ, the anointed One, and His anointing. I believe signs, wonders, and miracles are proofs to this generation that God is alive and dwells in the midst of His people. Jesus authorized signs and wonders to follow you every day of your life.

Jesus Himself used transformative power as proof of His identity:

*Now when John had heard in the prison the works of Christ, he sent two of his disciples, And said unto him, Art thou he that should come, or do we look for another? Jesus answered and said unto them, Go and shew John again*

*those things which ye do hear and see: The blind receive*
*their sight, and the lame walk, the lepers are cleansed, and*
*the deaf hear, the dead are raised up, and the poor have*
*the gospel preached to them.*

**—Matthew 11:2–5**

Jesus basically said, "If John's not sure about me, tell him about the display of power you just witnessed." Remember, the kingdom is not in word but in power. Beware of people who talk a lot but lack the demonstration. The Bible says the Lord backed up the apostles' words with a demonstration of power that couldn't be duplicated:

*And they went forth, and preached every where, the Lord*
*working with them, and confirming the word with signs*
*following. Amen.*

**—Mark 16:20**

Revelation 12:11 states, "And they overcame him by the blood of the Lamb, and by the word of their testimony." This scripture has great spiritual depth and insight. However, I specifically want to point out that it implies we overcome, by means of the sanctifying power of Jesus' blood and the proof of our testimony, for the benefit of others. This is why the Bible instructs us to follow those who through faith and patience inherit the promises. Men must see your exploits! Your life should lead others to Christ. You were made for signs and wonders. Proverbs 11:25 says that "he that watereth shall be watered also himself." And rest assured, there is a great reward for those whose light shines brightly in the midst of darkness and whose salt preserves the lives of men.

With this in mind, I want to encourage you. Jesus has transferred that same transformative power to you to do even greater works than He did (John 14:12).

## *Be Diligent*

You are a carrier of God's power. That power has its origins in the Holy Spirit who lives and abides in you. You already possess the power to speak to any mountain and command it to be removed, and it will obey you. Not convinced yet? You still don't like what you see when you look in the mirror? Do the circumstances seem impossible to change?

The remedy is diligence. Diligence is being "constant in effort to accomplish something; attentive and persistent in doing anything."[10]

What do you do when you face circumstances that refuse to change? Have you ever felt like there is no way out? You're not alone. Every believer will face challenges or circumstances that seem insurmountable and immovable. The answer is diligent faith.

Recall the story of the woman who had an issue of blood for twelve years (Luke 8:43–48). She heard about Jesus. What did she hear? Proofs, signs, wonders, and miracles. She heard about the transformative power He demonstrated. The instant she heard about Jesus and what He was doing, faith came. Remember, faith comes by hearing (Romans 10:17). Faith comes the moment you hear. Therefore, she said within herself what was possible. She created the context of her transformation by faith words and corresponding faith actions. Faith will always inspire action. Faith without works is dead (James 2:20). Despite risking her life by being ceremonially unclean in public, she fought through the crowds thronging Jesus.

What do you think fueled her faith? Every one of the thousands of people present wanted to get close to Jesus, but this woman was the only one who touched Him with her faith. I believe what set her apart was her diligence to tell herself over and over, "If I can just touch the hem of His garment, I will be made whole." Her earnest and persistent faith touched Jesus' clothes and was so strong, Jesus felt healing virtue drawn from His body. This demonstration of power had nothing to do with Jesus' faith. This was her faith that made a demand on the power of Christ. Again, she kept saying it over and over again. She was diligent in stating her expectation, despite the crowds surrounding Jesus, despite the fact that it was taboo for her to be in public while bleeding, despite the fact that things seemed like they would never change and that she would ultimately hemorrhage to death.

God sends His Word to deliver you out of all your destruction. Every Bible-sponsored deliverance starts with the Word. John 1:1 says, "In the beginning was the Word." Your salvation in every circumstance starts with you hearing a Word from the King. When this woman heard about Jesus, faith exploded inside her. His Word leads you to Him. She heard something that made an encounter with Him the answer. Her diligent faith made her repeatedly say the same things until she trained her mind to unleash the faith in her spirit—the faith she had received when she heard about Jesus. Her faith was an unstoppable force. Jesus confirmed this when He said to her, "[Your] faith has made [you] whole" (Matthew 9:22).

The woman was diligent, training and discipling her spirit to overcome the impossible. Any world-class track athlete will tell you that thousands of hours of disciplined training went into that one race that made him or her a world champion. You need to apply the same kind of diligence to your spiritual life.

## *The Root*

Let me add another component of faith that complements your diligence. Read the following scripture and notice how the Holy Spirit helps us understand how faith attacks your circumstances:

*And in the morning, as they passed by, they saw the fig tree dried up from the roots. And Peter calling to remembrance saith unto him, Master, behold, the fig tree which thou cursedst is withered away. And Jesus answering saith unto them, Have faith in God.*

**—Mark 11:20–22**

It says in verse 20 that the fig tree died from the root upwards. Would you like to guess how faith tackles your circumstances? From the root up. If you've ever pulled weeds from a flower bed, you'll notice they grow back if you don't pull them up by the roots.

Your faith tackles the problem at its roots, so it never grows back again. Circumstances don't matter. Faith always works from the root up.

If you have this understanding, you won't be moved emotionally when things, circumstances, problems, and challenges seem unchanged. Let me explain. The fig tree died the moment Jesus cursed it. It looked alive, but it was dead at the root! Your circumstance may look unchanged, but faith destroyed the roots. It's dead! Peter noticed the next day that the tree was dead, but Jesus knew the tree was dead the moment He spoke the word *cursed.*

The same is true concerning your situation. Keep speaking the Word and the expectation of that Word, just like the bleeding woman. Speak God's Word over and over until your thinking is transformed. Train your spirit until you're convinced that nothing moves you spiritually, physically, or emotionally but the Word of God. Now you are ready to release your faith.

You have to give constant effort to overcome the obstacles and distractions of life. There are certain things

God will not do for us. He expects us to pick up our crosses daily and follow Him (Luke 9:23). Poor effort, a lack of diligence, little or no self-control, and the like will always lead to self-destruction. That's not the devil. That's choice. You must make the choice every day to give your all until the end.

The Bible says we must endure to see the end of a matter (Matthew 24:13). Your story is not finished. Your circumstances only make your testimony more interesting. You are coming out on top. You are the head and not the tail. You are above only and not beneath. And I believe—wait for it—you will one day lend and not borrow!

## *Don't Settle*

Let's review a biblical example of poor effort and its consequences.

Off and on for decades, the nation of Israel had been oppressed by the kingdom of Aram. In 2 Kings 13, we read of the prophet Elisha in an interaction with Joash, the king of Israel:

> *And he [Elisha] said, Open the window eastward. And he [Joash] opened it. Then Elisha said, Shoot. And he shot. And he said, the arrow of the LORD's deliverance, and the arrow of deliverance from Syria: for thou shalt smite the Syrians in Aphek, till thou have consumed them.*

> *And he said, Take the arrows. And he took them. And he said unto the king of Israel, Smite upon the ground. And he smote thrice, and stayed.*

> *And the man of God was wroth with him, and said, Thou shouldest have smitten five or six times; then hadst thou*

*smitten Syria till thou hadst consumed it: whereas now*
*thou shalt smite Syria but thrice.*
—*2 Kings 13:17–19*


"Thou shouldest have smitten five or six times." Elisha indicates that if Joash had done things differently and put forth more effort, the final result would've been far more to his liking. However, as a consequence of settling for what was easier, the king received less than what was possible.

Just like in the case of King Joash, the residue of religion will convince you to settle at three strikes instead of five or six. Realize that this isn't a case of God determining the outcome but rather an individual's personal choice, corresponding effort, and diligence, or lack thereof. Stop blaming God for things you ultimately determine.

As an example, it is your decision if you want to start a business. It is your choice, not God's, to wait for the right conditions to start that business. He committed Himself to giving you the power to get wealth.

I believe God provides the opportunity and raw material, and you provide the initiative. That's why when you hear about someone else's testimony of business success, it can unleash a power to inspire you to take the initiative in your own life. Testimonies are designed to prompt you to action, not just to generate applause in recognition of God's goodness.

Unfortunately in the days and weeks after your inspirational moment, the initiative is often quenched and the realities of why your ideas won't work begin to confiscate the God-given motivation that the initial testimony birthed in you.

## *Our Advantage*

Let's tie religion into the context of this subject. Religion doesn't motivate; it fatigues. How? Religion demands performance, and performance will ultimately wear you out. It will remove the joy of serving God over time. Religion says, "Do this, and God will answer your prayer. Do that and He will bless you. He didn't move because you forgot to do this."

In reality, God's motivation is His unconditional love for you. This is why the following statement is so groundbreaking. Please take a moment to contemplate the next verse, and embrace its advantages over its Old Testament counterpart:

> *But now hath he obtained a more excellent ministry, by how much also he is the mediator of a better covenant, which was established upon better promises.*
> **—Hebrews 8:6**

You have already obtained a decisive advantage over every Old Testament saint. David, Joshua, Moses, Ezekiel, and every other person noted in the Old Testament of the Bible had to look forward in hope of One who would come. Our advantage is in the covenant in which we reside because Jesus has *already* come:

> *For if that first covenant had been faultless, then should no place have been sought for the second. For finding fault with them, he saith, Behold, the days come, saith the Lord, when I will make a new covenant with the house of Israel and with the house of Judah: Not according to the covenant that I made with their fathers in the day when I took them by the hand to lead them out of the land of Egypt; because they*

*continued not in my covenant, and I regarded them not,
saith the Lord.*

*And they shall not teach every man his neighbour, and
every man his brother, saying, Know the Lord: for all shall
know me, from the least to the greatest. For I will be
merciful to their unrighteousness, and their sins and their
iniquities will I remember no more. In that he saith, A new
covenant, he hath made the first old. Now that which
decayeth and waxeth old is ready to vanish away.*
**—Hebrews 8:7–9, 11–13**

Verse 11 makes two startling, revelatory statements.
First, it reveals that no one will need to be taught; second,
it states that everyone will know God intimately. How is
this possible?

According to the New Testament, the blood of Jesus
has destroyed every trace of sin in the entire universe (1
John 1:7). That includes you. To become born again, you
must receive God's great gesture of love, His Son, into
your heart. All your sins are washed away as though you
had never sinned. This is what God's grace does for us. It
allows God to interact with you and me as though we had
never sinned! Hence, where sin once abounded, His grace
now abounds much more (Romans 5:20)." The Holy
Spirit takes residence in your heart. Now no one with the
indwelling Holy Spirit will need to be taught. The Holy
Spirit is your teacher, who teaches through the five-fold
ministry gifts of apostles, prophets, evangelists, pastors,
and teachers for the edifying of the saints.

After your *new birth* the Holy Spirit comes to live
inside you, so you can know God and even have access to
the deepest things of Him. The shedding of Jesus' sinless
blood purged all sin from the known universe down to the
sub-atomic particles that make up all matter. Through
Jesus, we now have a doorway to God. The veil has been

torn top to bottom (Matthew 27:51). The way to God is clear and secure, and the price for sin has been paid in full. Now you can come boldly to the throne of grace to receive from God.

## *Stand Your Ground*

With the aforementioned truths in mind, take time to examine your daily habits. What you do every day is laying the foundation of your future. As you make the choice to examine your habits, listen for the voice of God and do whatever He tells you to do. Obey God's voice at all costs. Your obedience to God is better than any sacrifice you can offer Him. Worship cannot replace obedience. You can't pray away disobedience.

Obey God just like Elijah did. God will not fail you. You can trust Him in any circumstance. God cannot lie (Numbers 23:19)! Trust in the Lord and lean not to your own understanding but acknowledge Him in all your ways (Proverbs 3:5–6). As a result, He will direct you to victory in every situation. Let me reiterate, God cannot lie. It's not that He won't; He can't.

If you believe that God will direct you to victory, take your focus off your problems. Overanalyzing a problem is dangerous. You run the risk of knowing more about the problem than you know about God. I meet people all the time with the wrong stance about their day. I ask, how are you? This is going wrong, that is bad, the devil is busy, and so forth.

I'm not belittling the severity of anyone's situation, but the Word says, "And the earth was without form, and void; and darkness was upon the face of the deep. And the Spirit of God moved upon the face of the waters. And God said, Let there be light: and there was light" (Genesis 1:2–3). When God said, "Let there be light," He used faith to make His thought a reality. God in fact made light *be* real.

Faith was the substance He used to bring what He desired into the world. To get it out of Himself into the atmosphere, He spoke it. God said it with confidence and gave no consideration to how dark things were. In doing so, He gave no life to what He didn't want and gave authority to light to be. In essence, faith is used to make things be as they are currently in heaven.

Jesus took the same approach with a life-threatening storm: "And he arose, and rebuked the wind, and said unto the sea, Peace, be still. And the wind ceased, and there was a great calm" (Mark 4:39).

You cannot have what you are unwilling to say. What you say in the face of adversity will impact the outcome. I frequently teach the power of initial reaction. Your first words or reaction influences the outcome. The devil cannot read your mind. He is neither spiritual nor biblical. He should know less about the Word of God than you do. All his attempts to quote Scripture are corrupted. Ezekiel 28:17 says the devil's wisdom was corrupted by reason of his brightness. Consequently, he has no grasp of the truth; therefore he is at the mercy of truth.

Jesus said, "I am the way, the truth, and the life, no man cometh unto the Father, but by me" (John 14:6). When you speak truth, it eradicates any lie. Jesus is truth.

With God anything is possible if you can only believe (Luke 1:37). Let me restate that for clarity: with God, anything, anywhere, and at any time is possible. As a matter of fact, you have an unfair advantage over all your contemporaries.

We see this in the lives of the three Hebrews in Babylon (Daniel 1–3). Against all earthly odds, they stood out in Nebuchadnezzar's court. It was impossible to ignore them or deny them. They stood out because God's presence in their lives overwhelmed their opposition.

Be prepared to stand your ground for what is right. Right will prevail. Standing your ground is the Bible's advice in adversity. Read below:

> *Wherefore take unto you the whole armour of God, that ye may be able to withstand in the evil day, and having done all, to stand.*
> —***Ephesians 6:13***

Every believer will be subjected to this test. Can you stand? Can you endure? Pressure will produce one of two things in your life: faith or unbelief. Pressure helps reveal what is in you. God already knows, but from time to time He will allow you to be subjected to testing. You're not ready until tested.

Psalm 105:17–20 reveals this truth:

> *He sent a man before them, even Joseph, who was sold for a servant: whose feet they hurt with fetters: he was laid in iron: until the time that his word came: the word of the Lord tried him. The king sent and loosed him, even the ruler of the people, and let him go free.*

Everything you can purchase at a store has been submitted to some form of testing to prove its durability and its ability to perform as advertised. The same is true regarding you. What you are going through is just a test. Stand your ground. The evil day comes to everyone, but here's good news: whatever test you face has been thoroughly vetted by God. We possess the faith to overcome any situation, but often it's pressure that reveals that faith.

## *In Every Season*

Let's stop for a moment and assess. I trust you sense your faith being stirred. I've already prayed that something inside you is beginning to stir. Like a Monet painting, when you step back, you should see that all the little dots create a vivid picture of God's faithful plan taking root in you and promoting you to another level.

It's okay if your life seems a little disjointed at times. We all feel that way from time to time. Just know that every rainy season is making way for new things to grow in you. Without the rain, plants and vegetation won't grow. You need the snow in winter to blanket the ground. Just know that it's hiding spring's potential for a new beginning.

Learn to trust God through every season. His thoughts concerning you are good ones. He doesn't have anything in store for you that's harmful.

Bishop Merritt of the Straight Gate International Church wrote a book entitled *My Faith Is Taking Me Someplace*. One of the major takeaways I received from his book was this: the randomness we see is actually a clear picture to God.[11] At times I struggle to see the forest for the trees, but God does not. He has a bird's-eye view. My future is His past! I came to understand that faith is designed to take you to a specific destination and to overcome every obstacle along the way. Faith is not a process of trial and error. Faith is confidence in God's point of view about you and everything that pertains to you.

Not one small detail—"one jot or one tittle"—will change until His entire program is completed to perfection (Matthew 5:18). Jesus came as a sacrifice fulfilling the law and the prophets. God is so committed to relationship with you that He gave His Son. Such a sacrifice requires a personal response from us. Going through the motions of religion will not bring satisfaction. It's a personal relationship with Jesus that will bring you fulfillment.

In my personal introspection, I discovered *trying to be* was a problem. The world was broadcasting to me from birth what I wasn't, what I lacked, what I couldn't do, and the like. The devil's strategy also included a system of excuses for everything: wrong skin color, wrong side of the tracks, wrong school system, wrong social economics, wrong odds for success, wrong culture, and so forth.

Please hear me, I'm not denying these challenges are real. They are. However, when I open my Bible and read about Jesus, it becomes clear that He became man and experienced every disadvantage any human being has ever faced, is currently facing, or will ever face. Despite this, He triumphed over the devil and all of his forces. The Bible reveals what's truly possible. It provides the inventory of heaven. My rights as a son are clearly defined, and my faith is what manifests them.

As a born-again believer, you're not trying to be saved or trying to get to heaven. Faith in Christ has made you and me acceptable to God. Jesus is not ashamed to call you his friend (John 15:15). Your righteous status allows Jesus to share everything He knows and possesses with you.

- You're no longer trying to be sanctified (Hebrews 10:14).

- You're no longer trying to be righteous (2 Corinthians 5:21; 1 Peter 2:24).

- You're no longer trying to appease God (Romans 5:1).

- You're no longer trying to get to heaven (Ephesians 2:6).

Jesus made all these things possible for you. Your responsibility is to not only believe Jesus, but also be willing to receive from Jesus. He has empowered you to receive everything that He received.

Take a break right now from reading this book and say the name of Jesus out loud. Do you feel it? Be like the two blind men who called out to Jesus until they got His attention and caused Him, the blessed Potentate, to stand still (Matthew 20:29–34). All of those religious folks kept trying to shut them up, trying to follow protocol, and Jesus had someplace to go. But when you are desperate for God, He's there for you. He will come to you.

Jesus has no problem walking through a crowd to get to you. He'll step over this one and walk past that one to come see about you. Ask the man who sat by the pool of Bethesda with an infirmity for thirty-eight long years. When it's your time, it's your time. Unleash your faith. It is your time. Your encounter with this book confirms it.

CHAPTER SEVEN

# Government Rule

The kingdom of heaven is a theocratic form of government. Dictionary.com defines theocracy as: "a form of government in which God or deity is recognized as the supreme civil ruler, the God's or deity's laws being interpreted by the ecclesiastical authorities."[12]

The kingdom of heaven is a government and is not a religion. The kingdom of heaven is the most powerful kingdom the world has ever known. Neither Rome in all its glory or even the empires of Asia or Africa can compare to the splendor and power of God's kingdom on earth.

The ruler of this kingdom is Jesus. He is the King and not a president voted on by the populace. As King, He rules by birthright. His lordship is absolute, and He owns everything: all the people, land, gold, silver, and resources. His kingdom has no end (Luke 1:33). Every preceding empire has been destroyed by a more powerful empire. This is not the case with the kingdom of heaven:

*And he shall reign over the house of Jacob for ever; and of
his kingdom there shall be no end.*

*—Luke 1:33*


Every aspect of matter, space, and time is under Jesus'
authority. The word of His power holds every atomic sub-
particle in place. At His behest, everything is and shall
remain as His Word has declared it.

Jesus' motivation is love and compassion for all
humanity.

In His three-year ministry, Jesus restored a kingdom
that had been lost through sin (and death as a result of sin).
He restored it by His own death and subsequent
resurrection, which produced the life that now sustains
you.

Once a person is born again, he or she instantly
becomes both a child of God and a citizen of the kingdom,
possessing inalienable rights. The Bible, therefore, is the
constitution of our government. All rights and privileges
are clearly articulated by the Holy Spirit who dwells
within you. Ephesians 2:12 informs us that we have
become recipients of His commonwealth and the
blessings contained in our covenant of promise. Health,
wealth, protection, wisdom, wellbeing, and the like are all
ours now through Jesus, appropriated by faith. You're not
trying to be, you already are what God says you are: His
child, an heir, possessing an inheritance.

This proves you are not a servant. Servants are not
entitled to their master's inheritance. It is received solely
by birthright. This is why Jesus declared to Nicodemus he
must be born again (John 3:3, 5). You possess dual
citizenship through your new birth, which positions you
on earth while simultaneously seating you in heavenly
places in Christ. You bear the political rank of an
ambassador. Your mandate as an ambassador, from your
King, is to exercise dominion authority on earth through

the authority inherent to the name of Jesus. This truth is vitally important because whatever Jesus wants done on the earth is accomplished through His church.

Church is the institution through which we, as agents for King Jesus, work the works of God. His church has a singular task: to enforce the will of God on earth as it *already* is in heaven (Matthew 6:10).

With these truths in mind, you must grasp the realization that Jesus does not run the world! Jesus runs His church, which is in the world. As believers, we are in the world, but we are not of this world.

The church is the bride of Christ. He is completely responsible for it. Therefore, Jesus is the only qualified source to grow, nurture, protect, and provide for it. Mankind is not the source. Our dominion mandate from the Lord puts the earth and all its resources under the church's jurisdiction, just like God the Father has heaven as His jurisdiction (Genesis 1:28).

With this brief synopsis in mind, don't be surprised when people ask you questions like, "If God is so loving, why is there so much pain and suffering in the world?" The answer is simple: people sin and make unrighteous choices. People value money over God to the detriment of mankind. For many in power, greed has replaced compassion. People willfully serve money and not God. This is why it's so important that kingdom-minded people take their rightful place in the pillars of society to bring righteousness and justice back into favor.

## *The Role of Prayer*

Mankind was created to manage everything on earth. When God says "let them have dominion" in Genesis 1:26, we see that He turned over the rulership of creation to His offspring made in His image and likeness. From that time forward, the events of earth have been directly tied to the decisions that mankind makes.

God's words "let them" means His intervention on the earth is impacted by man's permission. By permission I mean prayer. Prayer gives God the covenantal right to intervene in the affairs of mankind.

This is why Jesus taught that we should always pray and not faint (Luke 18:1). Prayer gives God the right to intervene on earth. When you pray, the Lord of Hosts unleashes angels to assist you (Psalm 91:11). Every time you pray, angels that excel in strength come to your aid, loaded with provision and supply. Conversely, when you don't pray, God cannot respond, though He sees everything you're going through and every circumstance you face.

*For everyone that asketh receiveth; and he that seeketh findeth; and to him that knocketh it shall be opened.*
*—Matthew 7:8*

*And all things, whatsoever ye shall ask in prayer, believing, ye shall receive.*
*—Matthew 21:22*

Notice in both scriptures that everything is initiated by man. God sees and hears, but you must ask in order to receive; you must seek to find, and you must knock in order for any door to be opened.

Complaining is not praying, self-pity is not a defense, condemnation is not a strategy, nor is ignorance of God's Word an excuse. When a believer puts God in remembrance of His Word, in faith and confidence, things begin to happen. When your mouth begins to speak the Word, your change is on the way. Know that God is bringing His ability to your situation.

To prove my point further, let's look at Moses' commission to deliver the Israelites out of Egypt. God heard the prayers and petitions of His people who were being oppressed by the Egyptians:

> *And it came to pass in process of time, that the king of Egypt died: and the children of Israel sighed by reason of the bondage, and they cried, and their cry came up unto God by reason of the bondage. And God heard their groaning, and God remembered his covenant with Abraham, with Isaac, and with Jacob.*
>
> *—Exodus 2:23-24*

God saw every injustice His people were experiencing at the hand of the Egyptians. God reveals Himself to Moses and informs Moses that He has come down to deliver His people. Here's the key—God comes to deliver but He has to send a man—Moses—to bring the people out: "Come now therefore, and I will send thee unto Pharaoh, that thou mayest bring forth my people the children of Israel out of Egypt" (Exodus 3:10).

## God Needs You

I believe the theology that God doesn't need man is incorrect and has its origins with Satan. Additionally, I'm convinced any notion that minimizes man's importance on earth is satanic in nature. Science teaches that man was made (i.e., evolved) for the earth, but the Bible teaches that the earth was made for man! Mankind is the centerpiece of God's agenda to seed the universe.

Since God announced that He made man a little lower than Himself and put all the works of His hands under man's authority, Satan has worked relentlessly to devalue human life and its importance to God. We see this playing out in modern society, where there is little or no regard for human life. Kill a fetus, silence; kill a dog, outrage! This devilish theology is responsible for the religious concept that we are worthless, and God doesn't need us. How can that be true when God establishes the earth to be managed by mankind?

While it's true that God is self-sufficient and doesn't need mankind in order to exist, it is apparent, however, that God has determined He needs us for the purpose of relationship.

It was God's idea to make man in His own image. Why? For relationship. I believe your birth proves your worth! There was no need for you to be born if you didn't possess something needful for God.

The world's religious systems and apparatuses demand that you work for God's approval. The opposite is true. It is vitally important that you possess a proper sense of self-worth. That encompasses how you view yourself and how you perceive God views you.

You must see yourself as a son or daughter of God, not as a servant. Servants don't have the same rights, privileges, and access as a son or daughter of a king. Children have unabated access to their father, while a servant has to go through protocol to see his master. Relationship requires you to have the right perspective. Which relationship do you prefer; that of a child of a king or a servant of a king? This may seem counter to what you've been taught, but if God is your heavenly Father, then you are His child.

I realize it sounds spiritual to say I'm a servant of God, and I'm not criticizing you if you take that position. But can a servant come boldly into the presence of God unannounced? Esther 4:11 says that in biblical Persia, there was but one law: anyone, male or female, who came into the king's presence without being requested risked losing their life. This describes the protocol of servanthood. Servants are only needed to serve. Children are needed for relationship!

Having a wrong sense of worth regarding yourself or God can cause great harm to your mentality, specifically how you perceive your value in the world. You are valuable to God. He needs you for His will and purposes. God never intended for you to feel *less than*. On the contrary, we should exude a sense of being *more than* a conqueror through Christ who loved us (Romans 8:37).

When we read in Matthew 5:5 that the meek "shall inherit the earth," we need to understand that the word *meek* is referring to someone completely submitted to God's will and purpose for his or her life.[13] Jesus promises that these are the ones who will inherit the earth.

You have extreme value to God. Whatever He is going to do on the earth involves you. He has entrusted the Holy Spirit to dwell in you richly; this produces rivers of living water flowing out of your spirit. God intends for the kingdom in you to infiltrate and influence those you come in contact with. The Holy Spirit is working in your life through good times and bad, perfecting all the things that pertain to you, and His goal is the perfect formation of Christ in you, the hope of glory.

You're it. Settle right now in your heart that there will be things you will have to suffer through. Suffering for Christ produces obedience and creates a reservoir of compassion in your heart.

God is sovereign, but He chose to share His rulership with mankind. However, while mankind rules, God still retains ownership over everything seen and unseen on earth, beneath the earth, and throughout the cosmos. It's all His (Psalm 24:1).

## *Your Identity in Christ*

God intended from the beginning that man's rulership would function within the context of heaven's government. In this framework, man rules and God owns.

Man's relationship with God is only possible through faith in the death, burial, and resurrection of Jesus Christ. By grace through faith, a man is redeemed from sin, translated into the kingdom of Jesus, and takes unto himself a relational position of sonship, a country of origin, position of citizenship, and governmental position of ambassadorship. Let's examine how the kingdom of heaven defines each position through Scripture.

- You are not a servant but a son or daughter (Luke 15:21, 24; John 15:15).

- We are no longer illegal aliens but legal citizens of the kingdom (Ephesians 2:11–13).

- We've been reconciled to God and now hold the position of ambassador (2 Corinthians 5:19–21). That means all of the ambassador's credentials, expenses, housing, wages, transportation, health care, and family needs are paid for by the home country. In many countries today, the debts of their ambassadors are paid off so the ambassador can focus on his or her assignment. Did you catch it? This is a good time to give Him praise. If earthly governments provide for their ambassadors, what will your heavenly Father do? He owns everything.

Wake up today to the realities of who you are in Christ. Based on relationship, you are secure in His righteousness. I'm speaking to a son or daughter of God, a citizen of His kingdom, and a certified ambassador and emissary of Elohim.

*And in the days of these kings shall the God of heaven set up a kingdom, which shall never be destroyed: and the kingdom shall not be left to other people, but it shall break in pieces and consume all these kingdoms, and it shall stand for ever.*

**—Daniel 2:44**

*Of the increase of his government and peace there shall be no end, upon the throne of David, and upon his kingdom, to order it, and to establish it with judgment and with justice from henceforth even for ever. The zeal of the LORD of hosts will perform this.*

**—Isaiah 9:7**

I want to conclude this chapter by reminding you that history reveals that every form of human government will come to an end. Democracy and the republics that embrace it will end.

Conversely, the Holy Spirit declares that the kingdom of God will never end. It will ultimately destroy every earthly government in existence. By the time God is through, there will be no trace of those opposing governments. God has declared that He will see to it personally.

CHAPTER EIGHT

# Your Faith Level

Simply stated, faith is believing God. Your faith reveals the level of confidence you have in God. Every individual has a threshold, a plateau he or she has to break through to get to the next level. God expects you to use your faith to get to that level. The goal is a harvest. The goal is increase in your life. The Word falls on the good ground of your heart. When the Word takes root in your heart, the potential for harvest is unleashed.

There's an old saying: "Water finds its level." The same is true with faith. You can say, "I'm a person of faith." You can confess, "I have strong faith." However, faith will always find your threshold. Check the last battle. Examine the previous test. Did you pass or fail?

Faith will reveal the level of confidence you have in God. The circumstances of life are competing with your confidence in God. I want to help tip the scales in God's favor. I want to convince you that He can be trusted in any event. I want to inspire you to trust in God to the degree that it no longer matters if you win or lose; you trust God.

You break the devil's back when you no longer keep score. I mean, you no longer trust God just because you won. You trust in Him simply because of who He is. You melt away, along with all your cares. You lose your awareness of the difficulties you're facing for the safety of merely being with Jesus. It takes faith that's been put under enormous pressure to walk out of a spiritual scorecard mentality.

## *Matters of Faith*

I feel inspired, as I'm writing this book, to unpack some of my insights on the subject of faith. I want to take you into my thought processes of what I believe it really means to have faith in God. The following are a few questions I hope to answer: what faith is not and what it is, how it works, what makes it function, and what makes it malfunction.

### What Faith Is Not

Faith is not a conclusion you arrive at based on your perception through the five senses. To understand, let's look at Adam. When he named the animals, Adam operated at a level of faith so in tune with God's will that he named each creature by the name that God Himself would've named them. Faith empowered Adam to see God's reality! By faith, Adam's choice was God's choice. This is the supernatural nature of faith. Human reasoning can't do this, and human reasoning is what mankind was reduced to because of Adam's transgression.

When Adam ate the forbidden fruit (Genesis 3:6)—when he rebelled—he lost the life of God and became a dead spirit. He could no longer function in faith as God had originally intended. He and his descendants now had to provide for themselves. His world could only be perceived by his five senses. His ability to see, hear, touch, feel, and taste had become the extent of his reality.

This is what Adam was reduced to as a result of his rebellion against God.

At his best, unredeemed man is limited to conventional wisdom. Conventional wisdom has great value. Its foundation is rooted in education, which is good and very important. Conventional wisdom, education, and common sense all have value, but all are inferior to revelation. Man was created to live by revelation—revealed knowledge. Revelation is God's knowledge, understanding and insight springing up from within your spirit. It causes you to see things as God sees them. Without God, man is reduced to information originating from the outside. Information on the outside is accessible to anyone, but revelation is only accessible to the children of God. The things of God are spiritually discerned.

*But the natural man receiveth not the things of the Spirit of God: for they are foolishness unto him: neither can he know them, because they are spiritually discerned.*
**—1 Corinthians 2:14**

In my thirteen years of pastoring, I've observed that the perception of what is possible is limited to most people's natural senses. It's difficult for people to grasp their realities beyond what their eyes see or what they've experienced in the past. They don't see the unlimited world of creative power and potential that faith makes available.

If you choose to live by any means other than faith, you are a malfunctioning spirit, reduced to living beneath your privilege, which Jesus died and rose again to provide you. This point is worth repeating: *God has ordained you to live a lifestyle of faith.* This means we ought to live by faith day by day, not merely when problems arise.

**What Is Faith?**

Faith is that singular, spiritual substance by which all things in the natural, three-dimensional world exist. It is the raw material that God Elohim used to create everything seen and unseen. The proper application of this substance moves a believer beyond the limitations of natural ability into the supernatural realm where time and human frailties are no longer relevant.

By faith, you move beyond possible into the impossible. This is why you must know that faith is not experiential. Simply stated, God is creative. He doesn't do the same thing twice. You can't comprehend His next move based on what He did before. People who don't understand this live in the past, not in the now where everything God is doing is brand new. Faith comes by hearing (Romans 10:17), not by what has been heard! What you're hearing now is creating faith perfectly suited for today's challenges. This is why faith brings God pleasure. Jesus sought it with such fervency during his earthly ministry that those who displayed it greatly were immortalized by their stories being recorded in Scripture. Its relevance is so paramount that without it you can neither please God nor approach Him.

God used faith to create everything we see and everything we do not see. Faith is the spiritual DNA of creation and the basis of the success or failure of a man's life. The ramification of your *faith life* is so far-reaching that generations to come will be affected by your decisions today of whether or not you believe God. Please hear me—your children, your children's children, and every subsequent generation will be positively or negatively impacted by your use, misuse, or neglect of faith. Therefore, your understanding of faith should be practical and straight forward.

The best way for me to convey faith in the most

practical light is to reveal a portion of my own life's story that led me into full-time ministry. On March 23, 2008, my life radically changed. I received a call to return to the office for a mandatory meeting. When I arrived in the company president's office, I was informed that my employment had been terminated. Stunned, I asked why. I was informed that the decision was not based on poor performance but simply that the company could no longer afford me. At that time, I was a board member and executive director of operations with over 250 employees. I had a handsome six-figure salary with bonuses and company perks. In a matter of fifteen minutes, my twenty-five-year career in the automotive industry was over! I remember the long drive home and sitting in my driveway, trying to process what had just transpired.

I remember sitting in my car staring out the window at the new home my wife and I had purchased only fifteen months prior. I finally decided the best thing to do was to call my man of God, Bishop Andrew Merritt, for prayer. When I called him, I first wanted him to know that I believed God and that I had no fear regarding what I was about to tell him. Over the next twenty minutes or so I gave him the details of the most tumultuous day of my life. I told Bishop that I simply believed the Word would deliver my family. He prayed a powerful prayer, and I remember so clearly how I began to have this inner confidence that seemed to supersede the real challenges I faced: a large mortgage on a five thousand square-foot home; two children in private schools; a son about to go to college; not to mention a church that my wife, three children, and I had founded the year before, with about thirty members.

I made a decision by faith, right then and there, to walk away from anything that could compete with my call to ministry. I decided I would never work for anyone else and that God would be our total source for everything. It seems like a lifetime ago when I walked into the house trying to craft the words to tell my wife, but even more importantly, coming to grips with the decision that I was leaving corporate America for good and walking in my calling as a full-time pastor.

The Holy Spirit used that crisis to propel me forward. The pressure of that moment unveiled faith from within. Looking back on it now, I realize it takes pressure to make something valuable and priceless. It takes pressure to make diamonds. It takes pressure to make petroleum. It takes pressure to make you.

Your heavenly Father is passionate for all His people to harness the single most powerful force known to man, a force so overwhelmingly pervasive that absolutely nothing seen or unseen can destroy, alter, or diminish its properties. I'm referring to faith as a force precisely because of its unstoppable essence, an essence that has its origins in God. In the right hands and used skillfully, this force will vanquish any foe, overcome and overwhelm any obstacle, and transform the direst of circumstances. Most importantly, this force, properly applied, gives any human being access to God the Father, the Creator, and possessor of heaven and earth. It also gives us access to the eternal life of God.

Faith is a spiritual force, and like all spiritual things, though real, it is invisible. It is invisible to us in our three-dimensional world but visible and tangible in the realm of the spirit, the realm of the supernatural. Thus, it cannot be detected by the physical senses.

*Through faith we understand that the worlds were framed by the word of God, so that things which are seen were not made of things which do appear.*
**—Hebrews 11:3**

Faith is the means by which God has chosen to transfer humans into His family, the household of God. Ephesians 2:19 says, "Now therefore ye are no more strangers and foreigners, but fellowcitizens with the saints, and of the household of God."
Faithfulness ignites companionship with God and opens the channel of communication with Him, as we see in the life of Moses when the Lord says, "With him will I speak mouth to mouth, even apparently, and not in dark speeches; and the similitude of the LORD shall he behold: wherefore then were ye not afraid to speak against my servant Moses?" (Numbers 12:8). This means God spoke clearly and concisely to Moses.
Why did God choose to speak so intimately to Moses? The answer may shock you. As with any relationship, there are levels. With some people, you may have a purely cordial relationship, but with others, it may be more spiritually intimate. I believe God is revealing that faith is a pathway to intimacy with Him. The degree to which Moses trusted God thrust him into a level of closeness that granted close encounters with God.
This is an example of the level of relationship we should desire with the Father. Now you can see more clearly that faith is a key element that draws you closer and closer to Him. If you want more intimacy with God, believe His Word. If you want to see His ability manifesting in your life and working on your behalf, believe His Word. The natural result of knowing God is believing God. The result of believing God is obedience, and the result of obeying God is relationship.
Be careful to avoid the subtleties of Satan. He works hard to convince you to settle for what's reasonable. Satan doesn't fear the person who lives by a rational ethos. I'm not suggesting you live an irrational life. I'm saying the days of normalcy and living by human reasoning ended the day you became born again. Now your life has no

limits. Now faith in God has taken the proverbial lid off of what is truly possible in your life.

If you believe you will never succeed, you won't. If you believe your marriage will fail, it will. God will work on your behalf, but belief is a prerequisite. Notice in the following scripture that Jesus asks two blind men an interesting question.

*And when he was come into the house, the blind men came to him: and Jesus saith unto them, believe ye that I am able to do this? They said unto him, Yea, Lord.*
**—Matthew 9:28**

Men come to Jesus but don't necessarily believe. I'm sure you know people who go to church regularly, hear the same sermons you do, and request prayer. However, if you talk to them, you can quickly discern if they don't believe. Matthew 9:29 confirms this when Jesus says, "According to your faith be it unto you." It was their faith that activated healing in Jesus.

You must have faith that God is who He reveals Himself to be. That means He's your source for everything. He's your healer, deliverer, provider, restorer, life, health, and strength. The life that you now live is His life.

What made this all possible? Faith in God. Believing grants access. Unbelief denies it. Any believer who approaches God must approach Him from the perspective that he believes God can do whatever is needed.

How many times have you approached God in prayer, but wavered before you prayed, not sure if your request would be granted? That's unbelief. Satan probably flooded your mind with rational thoughts like, *"You're not good enough. You sinned last week, and God is still angry."* The devil uses perversion to convince you to embrace unbelief. Unbelief is faith in the kingdom of darkness. Faith is faith in the kingdom of heaven. Let's go back to the two blind men barging into Jesus' house to receive their sight. I'm sure it was difficult for two blind men to get to Jesus. However, their pursuit was rewarded. Jesus addressed their expectation for their sight to be restored. They did not need rehab, eye drops, or six weeks to recover. Instantly, their entire sight system was made brand new. When you go to God, you must believe that He can do exceedingly and abundantly above all you ask or think, and He will reward you for your diligent pursuit.

With so much emphasis given to faith, you may be wondering about love. What role does love play in the process of faith? Doesn't everything start with love? I'll attempt to answer this question as succinctly as possible. God is love. God is not faith. God, who is love, uses faith to express His love. Did you catch that?

*For in Jesus Christ neither circumcision availeth any thing, nor uncircumcision; but faith which worketh by love.*
**—Galatians 5:6**

God, who is love, uses faith to do His work. The same is true for us as God's offspring. If what you're doing to fulfill God's will in your life doesn't require faith, it's not from God.

You were created to thrive in the atmosphere of faith. To please God, you live life by faith, doing everything in faith. You wake up by faith. You go to work by faith. You plan by faith. You love others by faith. You receive healing by faith. You are forgiven of your sins by faith. Based on these statements, is it any wonder that God declares it futile to try to please Him without faith since faith is quintessential to your success in life?

Consider father Abraham. In Genesis 12, the Lord instructed Abram—his name before God gave him the name of Abraham—to "get thee out of thy country, and from thy kindred, and from thy father's house, unto a land that I will shew thee" (Genesis 12:1). Do you think Abram's decision to leave made sense to his family? I'm sure people who cared for him tried to talk him out of it. I could understand if Abram expressed some reluctance to take God up on His offer, but he didn't. He believed. His faith was demonstrated when he walked away from his father's house, inheritance, family, and friends.

I believe you will be given an opportunity to step out into the unknown and redefine your future. It will always cost you dearly when you put your trust in God. You may lose a few friends along the way. Some family members may question your common sense.

However, there's no turning back when you know He spoke to you. For some, trusting God may mean finally starting your new business and having to leave your job and the security of a steady paycheck. For someone else, it may be a difficult medical decision. For others, it may be finally stepping out of the background and confronting your anxieties.

Whatever it is, God makes it possible to accomplish your goals by faith. Without faith, we are reduced to our own intellect, personal experiences, and human reasoning that derives its impulses from the sense realm.

**How Faith Operates**

When Hebrews 11:1 says that faith "is the substance of things hoped for, the evidence of things not seen," it means that you can't naturally see, touch, feel, taste, or hear faith.

Faith is, in fact, the proof that we have the deed to what we are believing for. A deed legally signifies who has ownership of a possession. If you used your faith and paid off your thirty-year mortgage in ten years, the bank would give you the title deed to the property. If someone else were to say they owned the house, you would merely produce the deed that legally confirms you as the homeowner. The bank would support your claim because you have the title deed.

You may feel something when you step out in faith, but just understand faith is not a feeling. Any effort to lower faith to the natural level of your feelings is paramount to stepping out of faith and stepping into unbelief. It is unscriptural to say you believe God for something and the next day tell someone you hope it happens. Faith is the substance that represents what you're hoping for.

Don't be disheartened if you don't feel anything or if things seem unchanged. Faith itself is the proof you have what you're believing for, although at that moment, you can't see it.

Your belief system is the driving force of how you live your life. The Word of God works to alter how you think and, thereby, shape what you believe because you are what you believe.

You are a believer but so is everyone else, to an extent! Everyone believes in something. Atheists believe there is no God. Even the devil and his minions believe in God (James 2:19).

The difference is we believe that Jesus is Lord, and we submit to His righteousness. We were made to live a lifestyle of faith—the God kind of faith. When you became a believer, you were translated out of the natural form of living, limited by sensual perception and experiential inferences, into the optimal supernatural realm.

Now you live beyond what circumstances say is possible. The limits have been removed. You're convinced by what is written. No problem is beyond resolution. No hole is so deep God can't get you out of it. When you lean on Him and obedience to His Word, the realm of the possible is transformed.

Have you ever noticed you never limit what's possible in your imagination? In your imagination, you are free to see yourself as a great athlete or actor or executive. There are no limits. I believe that's what your heavenly Father wants you to receive from this book: freedom. You can obtain freedom to believe that things will change radically for the better for you and your family as your faith and your relationship with God grow.

As believers, we should have childlike faith, asking in accordance with His will and expecting to receive regardless of the situation and circumstances. If it is written, it is not only possible but probable. This is why Jesus states "for of such is the kingdom of God" (Mark 10:14). The kingdom has high regard for a childlike mentality of faith. Faith is not natural, but supernatural. It will never fade away. Faith is the supernatural means through which God chose to create everything. Every human being possesses human faith. Human faith is necessary in a natural world. Human faith engages the five senses in order to comprehend the natural environment.

However, the *God* kind of faith is supernatural. It doesn't need the assistance of your emotions or your five senses to confirm its reality. Only the God kind of faith pleases God! Human faith is not a substitute for what pleases God. You cannot satisfy the conditions of His Word through human faith, and I am convinced this is why many believers do not experience the fullness of the promises of God.

If you need evidence that God is in something, recognize that faith itself is the proof of God's involvement. God's fingerprint is faith! Faith is the evidence God leaves behind that reveals His involvement. God leaves His sovereign fingerprints in everything He does. The believer who operates in faith manifests the proofs God is involved. Faith performs feats that humans can't duplicate.

Glory to God! In Him we live, move, and have our very being (Acts 17:28). When you speak out God's Word, you sound like God. When you believe with His faith, you leave His fingerprints and get His kind of results. After all, isn't that what we're all after, His kind of results? It's easy math: human faith gets possible results; God faith produces impossible results. His faith is so infinitely powerful that a mere mustard seed-size portion of it can literally move any obstacle that stands between you and your destiny (Matthew 17:20).

Your circumstances are no match for the faith that is inside you. Trouble doesn't stand a chance against God. Let God arise and let all His enemies be scattered. Faith moves God!

Remember what I said previously: faith is supernatural. You need a supernatural means to deal with Satan and his wiles. By *wiles*, I mean his plans, attacks, strategies, plots, and deceptions. Regardless of the tactics he uses, his wiles are no match for you in faith. We are instructed to put on the whole armor of God (Ephesians 6:11–17), and the shield of faith is "above all" (Ephesians 6:16).

The word *all* is very important. All means all. All includes any economic recession, bankruptcy, investment downturn, or depression. All includes cancer, HIV/AIDS, dementia, diabetes, or high blood pressure. All includes every mental illness, state of confusion, or form of oppression. All includes any separation, divorce, or destroyed relationship. All means all! Faith is the remedy for every form of satanic attack or discomfort. Faith will release you from the pressure, stress, and anxieties that come with the cares of this life. Faith can withstand the pressure. Faith takes the pressure off you and places it on the Word of God. Instead of pressure, you experience His rest.

You must stand upon the Word as you walk in faith. The Word of God is designed to manifest the image that God has of you in heaven on earth. This is why God told Joshua to meditate on the written law day and night and not to depart from it (Joshua 1:8). God deemed study and meditation of His Word as the means for prosperity to impact a generation. He showed Joshua how to alter the hardwiring of his thinking to make him a success.

Abram, too, believed God's Word: "And he believed in the LORD; and he counted it to him for righteousness" (Genesis 15:6). God got Abram to look to the heavens. God created an image in Abram's mind that cemented His confidence in God.

Look at the link between faith and obedience. When a believer says, "I have faith in God's Word," yet refuses to obey the Word, that person simply deceives him- or herself. It's tantamount to getting in a new car and trying to start it without an engine. Faith requires active and deliberate obedience in order to function effectively and consistently.

God's eternal purpose in creating man and breathing His image and likeness into Adam's being was to share His rule and monarchy with His offspring. Adam was created to have dominion by faith. This means that Adam was designed to be fruitful by faith, multiply by faith, replenish by faith, and subdue by faith. For Adam to attempt rulership by any other means than faith would cause him to malfunction. God presents Himself to us in the same context of faith. Hebrews 11:6 says, "for he that cometh to God must believe that he is a rewarder of them that diligently seek him."

## *Obedience Through Faith*

God required obedience from Adam. Faith would

operate through Adam to fulfill his assignment as long as he obeyed God. If Adam disobeyed, he would die spiritually and naturally. There cannot be faith without obedience tied to it.

Elijah tells the widow of Zarephath to make him a little cake *first*, and *then* the miracle would come. Obedience through faith comes first—then the supernatural.

*And Elijah said unto her, Fear not; go and do as thou hast said: but make me thereof a little cake first, and bring it unto me, and after make for thee and for thy son. For thus saith the LORD God of Israel, The barrel of meal shall not waste, neither shall the cruse of oil fail, until the day that the LORD sendeth rain upon the earth.*
**—1 Kings 17:13-14**

Just like the meal and the oil flowed, faith should flow in your life. Faith requires your obedience to the direction of the Holy Spirit. He is the Spirit of truth. He will lead you to where the provision is. He knows where everything is on the earth and how to get it to you. As you release your faith and obey His holy direction, He will reveal supernatural supply. I have learned through experience that you need faith to endure the storms of life.

When I was younger, I viewed faith as a means to avoid or be delivered from the storms of life. I found out through experience, though, that the Holy Spirit doesn't always want me out of the storm. What He wants is my faith to flow *in* the storm. This is one of the ways in which we learn to trust and obey. It's *in* the storm that your faith is tried as silver and gold. It's *in* the storm that your obedience is perfected. God's will for you is that you come out of every test with your faith intact! This is only possible through obedience.

When Jesus bids Peter to walk on the water, He does

not calm the sea for him (Matthew 14:29). Jesus expects Peter to walk on water *in the midst of the storm*. Your faith will require stamina. The choice to obey Jesus and to step out of the boat was solely up to Peter. The storm was no more than a distraction. Walking on water was the miracle.

Faith causes us to see what God sees. It refines our focus to see the big plans of God. God wants you to believe His reality. His reality is His Word. Believing Him and His reality will put you at odds with the world. He brought you out, just like He brought Abram out of Haran. His plan is to bring you out to take you in!

Your passport to enter in is faith. You have to receive His reality by faith. This flow of faith will produce supernatural provision and increase. The truth is, you've been freed from the law of sin and death (Romans 8:2).

However, you must understand everything happens within the context of His divine will. You can't just be anywhere doing anything and expect the reality of blessing to overtake you. You must be in the position God has placed you, anticipating God's timing, doing the thing God has called you to do. Everything in your life is connected to God's righteousness and His sovereign agenda.

Think for a moment: Abram had to leave his father's house (Genesis 12:1). Moses had to tell Pharaoh to let his people go (Exodus 5:1). Elisha had to be in position when Elijah was translated into heaven (2 Kings 2:1–14). The disciples had to wait in Jerusalem until they were endowed with power from on high (Luke 24:49). Jesus had to endure the cross to redeem us back to the Father!

## *Faith and Financial Breakthroughs*

Let's examine the connection between faith and obedience that leads to financial breakthroughs. Read the following text carefully. I'm sure it's familiar to most, but there are a few principles I want to point out.

> Arise, get thee to Zarephath, which belongeth to Zidon, and dwell there: behold, I have commanded a widow woman there to sustain thee. So he arose and went to Zarephath. And when he came to the gate of the city, behold, the widow woman was there gathering of sticks: and he called to her, and said, Fetch me, I pray thee, a little water in a vessel, that I may drink. And as she was going to fetch it, he called to her, and said, Bring me, I pray thee, a morsel of bread in thine hand. And she said, As the LORD thy God liveth, I have not a cake, but an handful of meal in a barrel, and a little oil in a cruse: and, behold, I am gathering two sticks, that I may go in and dress it for me and my son, that we may eat it, and die. And Elijah said unto her, Fear not; go and do as thou hast said: but make me thereof a little cake first, and bring it unto me, and after make for thee and for thy son. For thus saith the LORD God of Israel, The barrel of meal shall not waste, neither shall the cruse of oil fail, until the day that the LORD sendeth rain upon the earth. And she went and did according to the saying of Elijah: and she, and he, and her house, did eat many days. And the barrel of meal wasted not, neither did the cruse of oil fail, according to the word of the LORD, which he spake by Elijah.
>
> —*1 Kings 17:9–16*

Let's examine five important truths from Elijah's story that unlock financial breakthroughs.

*1. The widow woman had the benefit of an encounter with a man of God.* Respect those in authority over you. I'm perplexed by believers who don't respect their pastors—the very people whom God has given the duty to watch over their souls (Hebrews 13:17). The Bible says you cannot hear without a preacher (Romans 10:14). You need a man of God in your life. My man of God is Bishop Andrew Merritt of the Straight Gate International Church.

Every opportunity I have, I sit with him and allow him to speak into my life. His words have transformed my life, and the same should be true regarding your pastor.

2. *The man of God has the God-given right to request of your resources.* Jesus asked Peter for the use of his boat (Luke 5). Peter obeyed. When Jesus had completed His teaching, He told Peter to launch out into the deep for a drought. Peter obeyed and inherited a boat-sinking miracle that financially sustained him, his family, and his business partner's family for years. When your pastor presents an opportunity to sow from your resources, don't hesitate. Your financial breakthrough is on its way.

3. *What will be asked of you will not make sense to your natural mind.* Follow the instructions given. Don't try to figure things out on your own. Understanding is not a prerequisite for faith. That means sometimes you'll have to believe before you understand. God's methods won't always make sense. His methods are designed to make faith.

4. *God doesn't need a lot to produce abundance.* God will use what you already possess as the catalyst for increase. This is exemplified in the story of the loaves and the fishes. In Matthew 15, Jesus asked how many loaves they had. Jesus took the five loaves and two fishes and fed a multitude. In another instance, the Bible teaches us that God told Gideon he had too many soldiers to fight the Midianites (Judges 7). God reduced the number of Gideon's soldiers from thousands down to three hundred. Gideon obeyed God's instructions and completely slaughtered the Midianites.

5. *Satan will use the spirit of fear to stop you from giving.* The fact that God will use what you already have qualifies every believer for supernatural increase. This should encourage you if you are experiencing lack. God will require you to give what's in your possession and ask you to trust Him to multiply it. When God speaks to you

to release your faith in response to His voice, Satan comes immediately to try to convince you to hold onto your seed. He knows that if you obey and release your seed, it will produce a harvest. He will tell you that you don't have enough to meet your need. He will tell you that your bills won't be paid, you won't be able to buy groceries, and anything else to convince you to walk in fear. Just remember, the devil is a liar! There is no truth in him.

## *Freely Given*

Please hear my heart when I tell you that faith in the Word of God is the answer to your problems today. No problem is too big or too small that your faith cannot be appropriated to address. Faith is an unstoppable, supernatural force that will dismantle all the plots and schemes of hell. The shield of faith you possess is empowered to stop, dismantle, and obliterate all the plans and strategies that Satan can conjure up.

Please understand that as a redeemed man or woman of God, you are the most powerful being on earth! Don't choke on this statement. It's your reality. It's your destiny. You are not a victim of circumstance. You are a son or a daughter of God! You have eternal life, the life of God running through your veins.

Every resource you need to fulfill your God-given purpose on earth has been freely given to you. The world is waiting for your unique gifts to be brought out in the open. Use your faith to step out of the shadows. It will take courage. You already possess your future. It just needs to be released by words of faith.

I remember when my wife and I started talking about having kids. I used to say I preferred to have all my children college-aged by my early fifties. I recall telling the Lord I wanted three children: a boy, then a girl, and then another boy. God gave me exactly what I asked for.

We first had a son, three years later a daughter, and then another son three years after that. I had faith that God could and would fulfill my desires.

We must have faith that God is able to answer our prayers, because "faith is the substance of things hoped for, the evidence of things not seen" (Hebrews 11:1). And if He doesn't answer them the way we hoped, we can rest knowing His plan is better than what we imagined.

You have His Word, you have position in His family, and you are blessed with every spiritual blessing heaven possesses (Ephesians 1:3). You are so rooted in Christ that no man can pluck you out of His hand (John 10:28–29). No weapon formed against you, your spouse, your children, or your family shall prosper (Isaiah 54:17). You have to believe that by faith.

So many believers have been taught religion. Religion disarms you. Religion magnifies the devil. When I was growing up, I use to hear the adults in my family read the newspaper and make comments such as, "The devil sure is busy." They should have said, "The devil is defeated, and I'm going to do my part to enforce his defeat." My recollection of church as a child is of having a greater understanding and awareness of Satan and sin than I did of Jesus and His righteousness. I was sin-conscious instead of righteousness-conscious.

Be confident. The earth is the Lord's. He is in control. Nothing is outside His vision, wisdom, and power. He has raised you up in Christ for such a time as this.

## *Believe God*

My wife and I have traveled to many parts of the world. We have led pool attendants to Christ, seen servers delivered after we shared our faith, and engaged in organic conversations about Jesus with fellow travelers. We've prayed for people on a beach in France. We've ministered to people on planes. You are anointed to enforce Satan's defeat everywhere you go. There is no hiding place for darkness. Light shows up. Darkness flees. You are now the light of this world. Shake yourself. Realize the power that resides within you to set someone somewhere free in Jesus' name. Imitate Jesus. Say what you want to happen, not how things appear, not what statistics indicate or what your family history reveals.

A few months ago, in an attempt to convince members of Kingdom Living Church to believe my words, I asked a doctor friend of mine to let me borrow the white coat that all doctors wear. To add impact, I also borrowed a stethoscope. I created a name tag and wrote the name Dr. Faith on it and went out to preach.

Why did I do this? To attack a certain mentality. A person goes to a doctor for his or her first appointment. The doctor walks in the room with that white coat on and with a stethoscope around his or her neck, and the person believes everything the doctor says. The person doesn't know the doctor personally, where the doctor went to school, or what kind of grades the doctor received. However, in the minds of most, the MD designation gives the doctor the right to speak a good or bad report into their lives. We give doctors the power to diagnose our medical problems we may not be able to see or feel, and we follow their directions for recovery. Getting to church on time is a problem for some, but they're never late taking their pills four times a day.

Several years ago, my mother was diagnosed with a terminal stage of lung cancer. She undertook several months of intense chemotherapy but did not improve. The doctor told my brother and me that we needed to make her as comfortable as possible because she only had a month or two left to live. My brother respectfully told the doctor that we appreciated his efforts, but our mother was not going to die! We prayed right there in front of the doctor that she would live and not die. My brother took my mother off ninety-five percent of her medications. We brought her back to the doctor three months later. My mother had gained back all the weight she had lost. She looked so amazing that the head of cardiology said in all the years of his practice, he had never seen a patient improve so quickly.

What extended her life expectancy? Faith. There is a limit to what men can do. I believe faith begins when the strength of men ends. Be encouraged. Jesus can heal. His anointing to heal and deliver the oppressed is still working through His church.

I want you to understand that no situation is hopeless. Hopeless people are helpless people. Faith only gives substance to things hoped for, so faith will never exceed your capacity to hope. Satan strategizes to create thoughts of hopelessness in the minds of God's people. So be hopeful in all circumstances because your faith is working tirelessly to produce manifestation.

I believe God's people are to be supernaturally optimistic. We know with men, some things are impossible, "but with God all things are possible" (Matthew 19:26)! Resist all satanic urges of pessimism—they are designed to dismantle your hope in God. Remember, "to the pure all things are pure" (Titus 1:15 ASV).

As I stated earlier, all impossibilities are deceptions authored by Satan to convince you to believe a lie. Nothing is too far gone for Jesus and His anointing. Didn't He raise Lazarus from *the dead* (John 11:1–44)? For the anointing of God to flow in your life, it will require you to "take away the stone" (John 11:39) that blocks your understanding. Inaccurate teaching and religious traditions have stifled the power of the anointing from exploding in the lives of God's people. God wants to transform your life into a Garden of Eden experience, but this can't happen until you are willing to accept God's reality for your life. His reality is your purpose. Fulfill it by faith. If you can believe the Word, you will see the glory of God.

Thank God for what He did for you yesterday, but expect Him to exceed your expectations for today. If your last testimony you can recall was six years ago, something is wrong. I have learned through study and application that everything in God is designed to get better and better. There are no diminishing returns in God. None. Not one. Relationship with God, not religion with God, is designed to enhance your life over time.

## *Faith Comes from Trust*

Please remember, everything in the kingdom of heaven, on earth, is designed to make things better and better. Let me list just a sample of those who by faith have their exploits recorded in Scripture:

- Abraham went from a sun worshipper to a possessor of heaven and earth.

- Isaac went from being stuck in a famine-stricken land to ultimately becoming so rich he intimidated a nation.

- Jacob went from being a known hustler to becoming a financial giant.

- Moses went from a convicted murderer to a deliverer of a nation.

- David went from being a shepherd to becoming the King of Israel.

God is God. There is no other God beside Him. He has

an infinite range of choices in which to reveal you to the world. However, He chooses to move, He expects you to believe to see it manifest.

I trust the words of this book are speaking to you intimately. I pray that you engage this book with such fervor that God unleashes a rhema word that pulls up by the root every form of ignorance of God's Word inside you, particularly things that pertain to faith.

Develop the faith habits now that shape your future. When you leave this earth and a minister eulogizes your life, let the minister's testimony be that you lived a full life of *faith extenders*. Faith extenders are events or milestones in your life in which you passed the test and God took you to the next level of faith. Daniel went to the next level when he passed the lion's den test. The three Hebrews passed the fiery furnace test and were promoted. They didn't win because they were somehow superhuman and predisposed to believe God.

I believe they were just like you and me. I'm sure they were nervous but resolute. Their faith was put to the test under the most trying conditions. However, they won because of their love for God. It wasn't about living or dying to them but loving their God and being loyal even unto death.

What are you willing to endure in order to have a relationship with God? Are you willing to die for your convictions? Personally, I believe your relationship with your heavenly Father takes on an intense form of intimacy when it no longer matters how things turn out. You no longer love Him for what He can do for you but simply because of who He is. You stop being the issue. He becomes the center of everything. Success in faith is no longer measured in wins and losses but in trust.

Such trust is earned. You learn to trust God through adversity. He gains your confidence when you give Him a chance to prove to you that He is who He says He is.

Adversity that is the result of faith in God is the most fertile soil for growth. I want to encourage you. You are closer to your breakthrough moment than you think. A weight that may seem too heavy to endure from your perspective is called *light* in the Bible. A problem that seems like it will never end from your perspective is called *momentary* in the Bible (2 Corinthians 4:17). Faith requires you to agree that the Word is true, though, for a season, things may look and feel contrary.

It is vitally important not to panic when you fail in your pursuit of God. Notice I didn't say if you fail, but when you fail. We will all experience failure in our journeys with God. Experiencing failure doesn't make you a failure—lack of trying does. It is better to try and fail than to be too afraid to try. Peter walked on water, but he started sinking before he reached Jesus. Yet we celebrate that he at least stepped out of the boat, on faith, when eleven other men were too fearful to do so.

Please understand when I say the following: failure is inevitable. Everyone fails at something at one time or another. God knows how to use your failure to manifest winners. The Bible speaks to your response to failure: "For a just man falleth seven times, and riseth up again: but the wicked shall fall into mischief" (Proverbs 24:16).

This is where confidence plays a key role in the lives of those who prosper. You see someone on the cover of a magazine. You marvel at how good that person looks and how successful he or she is. However, you have to read the background story to learn that he or she lived in their car for three years, trying to survive, waiting for that breakthrough opportunity. The Word builds your confidence in God. These biblical truths will help you to prevail in your walk of faith.

## *Knowledge Is Greater Than Feeling*

In the kingdom, knowing the truth gives you an advantage over others. Knowing will always trump feeling. Feelings are important but fleeting. As we read in 2 Corinthians 4:18, our focus must remain on the unseen: "While we look not at the things which are seen, but at the things which are not seen: for the things which are seen are temporal; but the things which are not seen are eternal."

You build your confidence in God by spending time with Him, reading, meditating, and confessing His Word. Things may look challenging, but your confession of faith will put pressure on your circumstances to change dramatically. I know confidence is building in you as you read this book because confidence was growing in me as I wrote it.

God plans to fulfill His promises to you. Not a single promise of God will ever fail. We must meet the condition of the promise, and then the outcome is assured. Believe God, not the problem. When God speaks, everything changes. Put yourself in position to hear His voice. His voice is both tantalizing and irresistible. It will ignite the eye of your spirit to see what others cannot see and say things no one but you has the courage to say. You will start to decree things to define the context of your victory, just like the woman with the issue of blood.

I'm convinced the words of this book are fuel for future exploits in your life. As you read each page, you are gaining steam and momentum for the miraculous. Only believe. You've come this far by faith. There's no turning back now.

I believe the best is yet to come. I'm convinced we haven't seen the best of what God has in store for His people. Study faith to maintain a healthy attitude. Look at your attitude as a thermometer. A thermometer will tell you the temperature of your body. Faith does the same thing for us. It reveals how hot or cold we are spiritually. And your tongue is the key to faith. Faith is a spirit; it demands a confession.

According to 2 Corinthians 4:13, "We having the same spirit of faith, according as it is written, I believed, and therefore have I spoken; we also believe, and therefore speak." It's mandatory to fill your spirit with faith because your spirit is what God uses to bring forth good things:

> *A good man out of the good treasure of his heart bringeth forth that which is good; and an evil man out of the evil treasure of his heart bringeth forth that which is evil: for of the abundance of the heart his mouth speaketh.*
> **—Luke 6:45**

Faith conquers what may seem unconquerable. Faith in God is economy-proof. Faith in God renders race irrelevant. Faith in God has no respect for social status or education. Please don't misunderstand what I'm saying. Get an education, work hard, save your money. But just in case you're looked down upon because of your skin color or you didn't go to the best school or you didn't know the right people, rest assured that faith will get the job done. I'm a witness. How does an African American male from River Rouge, Michigan, with a 2.7 GPA, become a CEO of a multi-million-dollar company and ultimately receive the elevation to pastor in the Lord's church? By the grace of God. This same grace is sufficient for you (2 Corinthians 12:9).

Don't talk yourself out of your destiny. Stop talking about doing it, and just start moving. You can only obtain what you have the courage to move toward. God told Moses, "Every place whereon the soles of your feet shall tread shall be yours..." (Deuteronomy 11:24). If you're waiting until everything is perfectly aligned, you run the risk of missing God. Don't worry. The Holy Spirit will inspire you. He will go so far as to inspire others to inspire you. He is a quickening spirit. He will quicken (inspire) you to get moving toward your dream. And your faith is ready to serve you! Angels are on standby, waiting to hear you say something and see you do something.

## *When in Doubt...*

What if it doesn't work? What if I lose everything? What do you do when the unexpected happens? These are all valid questions. Let's see how David handled similar circumstances. David and his men were away, and their camp was attacked by an enemy who stole everything. Sounds just like what the devil is trying to do to all believers. David was devasted, depressed, and distressed. What did he do about it? He went to God for a strategy that empowered him to regain everything that was lost. That's what you must do, too.

> And David enquired at the LORD, saying, Shall I pursue after this troop? shall I overtake them? And he answered him, Pursue: for thou shalt surely overtake them, and without fail recover all.
> —*1 Samuel 30:8*

I want you to meditate on the following action items. I gained them from the scripture you just read. These action items are designed to positively impact your mentality in times of loss and distress. They will help you to pursue, overtake, and recover everything the devil has stolen, just like they did for me.

• Anything worth having is worth pursuit.

- You are disqualified from obtaining what you will not pursue.

- To reclaim anything lost takes tenacity and endurance.

- Don't get ahead of God. He puts everything in twenty-four-hour increments for a reason; focus on today.

- Nothing can stop your faith but you.

- Tell yourself things are going to be different from this day forward.

- The fact you woke up today means God is giving you another chance.

- Remind yourself that every day is full of untapped potential.

- Ask God to help you see what you haven't seen before.

- Be ready to go in a different direction if necessary.

- Be prepared to stop past practices and be ready to go in a new direction.

The faith of God inside you can help you regain your dignity, self-respect, self-love, and integrity. I can tell you from experience, what is regained will be better than what was lost.

Appreciation for your uniqueness from others will grow exponentially. Your witness for Jesus will exude the anointing of Christ. Value will be applied to things most take for granted, and compassion for others will increase. What the devil meant for evil will be transformed into good. So, if you've lost a lot, expect to love a lot.

Additionally, your current and past pain is sometimes a window into your future ministry. A man who struggles with his sexuality is more likely to listen to a man who was delivered by God's power from the same form of oppression. Pain births passion and compassion. Again, it's hard to fully appreciate your dignity until you've lost it to pornography; the shame can cause people to destroy their marriages and lose their children.

However, God is ready to restore you today. He loves you in spite of you. He is ready to make you whole again and reveal the gift of restoration of others inside you. Faith will activate you to action. Only believe God. If David had not pursued what the Amalekites had taken from him, he never would've reclaimed it (1 Samuel 30:1–19). Losing or winning is a choice. Using your faith will shape your mentality. A boldness and intensity to trust God under any condition will overtake you. Realize it's not over until you win.

God's boldness is already inside you. Release it by confronting the fear of moving forward in the thing the devil is telling you that you can't do.

## *In the Deep*

Let's look at another aspect of faith. Jesus told Peter to launch out into the deep and let down his nets (Luke 5:4). There are certain things you can only obtain in the deep. However, you can't see what's possible in the deep with the naked eye. You have to let down your nets to catch anything in the deep. You don't need faith in the shallow waters of the seen; you need faith for the deep waters of the unseen.

Look at your faith as the ship Peter possessed. God uses your faith. Your faith is the substance of things hoped for. Heaven interprets your faith as proof you trust God and His Word.

There will come a time when you will have to override your experience and human reasoning to receive what God has for you. In Peter's day, fishermen didn't fish during the day because the fish could see the net. That's why they had toiled all night (Luke 5:5). They toiled all night but caught nothing. This informs us that human strength can't compete with the potency of faith.

I have observed in the lives of people at Kingdom Living Church how faith has no regard for earthly systems. People have gotten jobs they weren't qualified for, and they've thrived at them. One family at KLC was approached by strangers who said, "We saw your house as we drove down the street and want to buy it." Their house wasn't on the market. There was no sign out front. But they were thinking about putting their house on the market because they needed more space. God knows what you're thinking before you think it. He wants to give you the desire of your heart if you will only believe.

In the aforementioned situation, God did what He often does. He overrode the rules and procedures of men—in this case through the buying and selling of real estate. The strangers bought the family's house for more money than the family expected and paid cash. No agents were involved, so no commission had to be paid. The family from KLC bought a new house, with more than enough space, in a beautiful subdivision. They were able to sell their house and buy a new one in roughly sixty days.

Faith can find abundance in situations where earthly systems see scarcity. The key is God's Word. Do what He tells you to do. Learn to wait on His voice.

Can you stand to be blessed? Release your faith. Listen for the voice of God. Obey what He tells you and get ready to receive. It doesn't matter what it is: all things are possible for those who believe (Mark 9:23). God knows how to exceed all your expectations. He knows your prayer requests before you ask Him. Therefore, we can conclude that God alone is qualified to take care of you, your family, and everything that pertains to you. He simply needs you to trust Him.

You may be asking, "How do I know if I trust God?" The tests of life will reveal the strength or the weakness of your faith. You can declare how strong your faith is, but often the storms of life reveal the foundation on which you stand (Matthew 7:24–27). Don't always assume sin is the reason for the challenge you may be facing. Sin didn't put Joseph in the pit—God did! The Bible says the Word of God tried him "until the time that his word came" (Psalm 105:19). When that time came, the king released him "and let him go free" (Psalm 105:20). It's the trying of your faith that perfects you and ultimately brings glory to God.

Our victory over the world is sealed by faith. Faith never fails. It never falters. It is the one thing you possess that terrorizes the devil. When you lift the shield of faith, you can quench every fiery dart of the wicked one.

## *Live by Faith*

The Bible makes it clear that the justified ones live by faith. Over and over again, the Holy Spirit documents the standard of our lifestyle as believers. We live by faith continually:

- "Behold, his soul which is lifted up is not upright in him: but the just shall live by his faith" (Habakkuk 2:4).

- "For therein is the righteousness of God revealed from faith to faith: as it is written, The just shall live by faith" (Romans 1:17).

- "But that no man is justified by the law in the sight of God, it is evident: for, The just shall live by faith" (Galatians 3:11).

- "Now the just shall live by faith: but if any man draw back, my soul shall have no pleasure in him" (Hebrews 10:38).

You already possess the victory over the world and all its temptations. Jesus has given us absolute and complete victory over Satan and his kingdom. All of our sins have been abolished. Jesus nailed our guilty sentence on His cross. Our death penalty has been canceled. Now through Him, we have absolute victory. Now, if God is for you, who can stand against you (Romans 8:31)?

Armed with His presence, His faith, His anointing, His kingdom, His Word, His nature, and His authority, you are an unstoppable force in the earth. You possess the God kind of faith. Speak His reality by speaking His Word. What God has for you is reserved in heaven, waiting for a demonstration of faith. Faith is the title deed that His promises are yours and stands as proof you believe God.

CHAPTER NINE

# What Is Good?

God is good. In most churches, when you say, "God is good," the response is, "All the time." He is a good God. It's human nature to project our own individual definition of good on God. However, I discovered something in Scripture that altered my thinking regarding the goodness of God.

> *And, behold, one came and said unto him, Good Master, what good thing shall I do, that I may have eternal life? And he said unto him, Why callest thou me good? there is none good but one, that is, God: but if thou wilt enter into life, keep the commandments.*
> **—Matthew 19:16–17**

A man asked Jesus a reasonable question: "What must I do to have eternal life?" For ministers of reconciliation, this is low-hanging fruit to win a soul for Jesus. However, Jesus first addressed the man's salutation. Jesus seemed to be more concerned with the title the man placed on Him than with his question about receiving salvation.

Jesus made clear that the only One who determines

what is good is God. He alone possesses the right to define what is good in your life. You've heard the saying, "What *looks* good may not *be* good for you." It's true. God is your maker. He knows what's best for you under every circumstance. God's Word defines what is good. You cannot. All goodness comes from God who resides in heaven (James 1:17).

God determined to give His people a good land, a specific location that He had reserved for them. Not just any land would do. Only the good land He chose, which flowed with milk and honey, was purposed for them. It's not that the land of Canaan was the only good land. It's that God reserved the right to determine what land was good for the Israelites. We know other land was visually beautiful because God warned Israel not to try to take it for themselves (Deuteronomy 2:5).

You may be asking yourself, "How do I know what is good for me?" The Bible identifies in clear terms the boundaries of what is good and not good for you.

For example, it's not good for you to have sex before marriage. Sex is good, but it's not lawful unless it takes place within the confines of the marriage covenant. There is no scenario where God permits premarital sex.

Why? God made you. He doesn't want you to have any bad memories. He knows that every time you get in the bed with someone you're not married to, it activates a physical and spiritual connection. This connection embeds images and desires in your mind that you will carry for a lifetime.

Second, sexual sin is a sin against your body. Remember, your body is the temple of the Holy Spirit (1 Corinthians 6:18–20). Sexual sin shortens your life expectancy. Third, God wants to save you from unplanned pregnancy. Many people think *I'll just do it this one time*, but it only takes one time to alter your life. You can be forgiven for sexual sin if you repent, but the image remains—or the baby is coming.

The blood of Jesus can wash away every trace of sexual sin, but you will have to live with the consequences. Unfortunately, you can't go back in time to undo past mistakes, but I can encourage you to demonstrate self-control, which is a fruit of the Spirit (Galatians 5:22–23). Repent for past mistakes and determine to only partake in what God says is good for you.

If you let God dictate what is good in your life, you will live a regret-free life. Your past won't have the power to hold you down. We all miss the mark from time to time, but we don't all need to have major regrets in life. The only way to ensure this is to let God be God. Let Him determine what is good for you.

The devil will always attempt to entice you. Even things you have overcome will be tested from time to time to validate if you still have the victory. You can be healed, but you must maintain your healing. You can be set free, but you must maintain your freedom. In every case, you must believe God.

You have to believe God. The devil doesn't give up because you confess the Word. His aim is to put pressure on you to lie, steal, fornicate, manipulate people, live in fear, and so on.

Our victory is rooted in love for God, who cannot change (James 1:17). We see society altering the laws to reflect changing attitudes about what is right and what is wrong. Why is homosexuality wrong if two people love each other? Why shouldn't we legalize marijuana since it comes from a natural plant? Why can't we live together before we get married to make sure we're compatible? These are a few of the questions we see debated today. There is no debate. What the Bible commands is truth. Everything else is deception. It might look good. It might feel good. It may sound good. However, if God says it's not good, that settles it. Let God be true, but every opinion, every human justification be a lie. Let God be true in every aspect of your life.

God alone is good. He alone possesses a monopoly of what is good and what is good for you. If you abide in His Word, you will comprehend the good things of Him (see John 15:7).

## *Wait on God*

Even things that seem bad to others can be deciphered as good through the Holy Spirit. He is sanctioned to lead and guide you to all truth. He will only lead you to what He deems good. Let the Holy Spirit speak to you. Look for His peace. Ask Him and you will receive His answer in a way you can perceive: a confirming word from someone, a revelation through Scripture, an uncomfortable feeling you cannot shake, or a comment from the preacher that seemed to speak directly to your situation.

If you don't know what to do, wait on God. Don't presume. It's always best to wait when you're not sure. However, waiting on God requires faith, just like everything else in Scripture. Consider how Abraham waited—but in faith. "He staggered not at the promise of God through unbelief; but was strong in faith, giving glory to God" (Romans 4:20).

Abraham believed God, and God credited him as righteous (Romans 4:3). What is it that God deemed so profound that He christened him the father of faith? Abraham believed that God would give him a son. Here's the catch—Abraham had to wait twenty-five years! God decided it was good for Abraham to have to wait for twenty-five years to receive the manifestation of His promise.

What is good? Let God decide. And then believe Him, in faith.

# CHAPTER TEN

# Godly Confidence in Yourself

Faith is the foundation of your confidence. The degree to which you walk by faith is proportional to the level of confidence you have in God. This book is structured to strengthen your confidence in God.

How do you strengthen your confidence in God? Systematically put things, namely your life and its experiences—past, present, and future—in perspective. It's easy to lose perspective. Wrong perspective can convince you that you're the only person going through what you're going through. Wrong perspective will convince you that you're alone and that nobody cares.

The only solution for a wrong perspective is to present the right perspective, the Word of God. This is what this book is methodically doing to you as you read it. It's forcing the lies of the devil out in the open. In effect, the light is dispelling the darkness. Let me explain it this way.

When you filter your past life through the Word of God, you realize your past is over and you merely learn from it.

When you filter your present life through the Word of God, you realize all of the benefits that are available to you right now. You combine the lessons learned from your past and the benefits and potential in today, and it causes you to rejoice and be glad.

When you filter your future through the Word of God, you reap the harvests of the lessons of your past and combine them with the previous benefits and opportunities you took advantage of, laying the foundation for a rewarding future. Your encounter with your wealthy place is inevitable. Faith is the substance of that inevitability. Faith is proof you will finish strong.

*Better is the end of a thing than the beginning thereof: and the patient in spirit is better than the proud in spirit.*
**—Ecclesiastes 7:8**

People may be critical of you now, but just wait. There is a day coming when they won't be laughing, but rather congratulating you. So be confident in the God in you. Your past is over. Unleash your faith in what's possible today and watch confidence rise in you like a well of living water, inspiring you and encouraging others.

## *Be Confident*

Confidence is key. First, be confident in yourself. For some, the notion of self-confidence is viewed as a lack of dependence on God. Nothing could be further from the truth. I believe a misunderstanding of Romans 12:3 is the reason:

*God has given me grace to speak a warning about pride. I would ask each of you to be emptied of self-promotion and not create a false image of your importance. Instead, honestly assess your worth by using your God-given faith as the standard of measurement, and then you will see*

*your true value with an appropriate self-esteem.*
*—Romans 12:3 (TPT)*

Here's the key: don't think too highly. Think highly, but don't overvalue yourself. With this in mind, you'd better have confidence in you, because God does. He has invested His best in you. I'm not a betting man, but I view this as God laying everything on the line that you will overcome victoriously. Trust that the greater One dwells within you. Your confidence is not based on your ability but on His ability working in you and flowing out of you to fulfill His purposes on earth.

I tell people all the time, your birth is proof God needs you for His plan. No one is born without a God-given purpose. No one is born without the potential to solve problems on earth. The uniqueness of you is what distinguishes you for destiny.

Unfortunately, few people comprehend their God-given purpose for living. They get stuck working a job they hate, desperate for a distant retirement, living in Monday, longing for Friday. This is not the way God wants you to think. He wants you confident that Monday has as much supernatural potential as the next day.

Use your faith to define every day as a milestone of faith. Let today be the day of salvation. Be free today of every sin that so easily besets you. Scatter the little foxes that hinder you from your true aim, which is to seek His kingdom and His righteousness. Allow God to add to you hour by hour, and day by day. See what the sweet psalmist, David, had to say:

*This is the LORD's doing; it is marvellous in our eyes. This is the day which the LORD hath made; we will rejoice and be glad in it.*
*—Psalm 118:23–24*

Now make your declaration of confidence in God, your heavenly Father, your provider. He is just as much your provider as He was to Abraham.

Colossians 1:27 declares that Christ lives *in you*, not outside you! Christ in you, the hope of glory. Be confident in the living God inside you. His presence is bigger than any problem. His presence in you makes the devil tremble. Your citizenship in the kingdom of heaven has granted you glorious rights that you must take advantage of.

## *Declare His Word*

Use your faith to declare His Word. Use your faith to say something impossible and make your today the destination for a manifestation. This day is a day of salvation. Be confident. Angels are on standby for something to come out of your mouth. God is so intent to make your today memorable, He's stated His readiness to answer you before you ask (Isaiah 65:24). Did you comprehend what you just read? God is ready to bless you before you speak. Your spirit is so full of God's reality for your life. Let your imagination conjure up something that your ability can't do. Listen as the Holy Spirit enlightens a scripture buried in your heart and thrusts it to the forefront of your mind. See your words as a revealing of your new reality. Don't ask your body for permission. Don't consider anything that opposes you. Encourage yourself with what has been written. Remember, your faith starts where your ability ends.

God will never ask you to do something you cannot do by faith. Only be strong and courageous (Joshua 1:7). Make up your mind to *be* what God commands. It's a choice. Don't you feel your confidence growing as you read these words?

In Joshua 1:6–8, God tells Joshua to be courageous; then He gives promises and finally He instructs Joshua to listen to and obey the law. Notice success isn't determined by God. Success was determined by Joshua expressing strength and courage no matter what happened. Human strength and courage are enhanced by meditation on and dedication to the Word of God.

In heaven you are already a resounding success. In heaven you're complete, seated in Christ. God has given you the measure of His faith to grow and nurture and to empower you to daily manifest heaven's reality on earth.

Whether you are newly saved or a bishop of a large international ministry, it doesn't matter. Something good is happening inside you right now. Receive it right now in Jesus' mighty name. Be confident in God. He has the power to master any earthly circumstance. Anything that pertains to life and godliness is subject to God and, by proxy, subject to you.

> *May grace and perfect peace cascade over you as you live in the rich knowledge of God and of Jesus our Lord. Everything we could ever need for life and complete devotion [a life of godliness] has already been deposited in us by his divine power. For all this was lavished upon us through the rich experience of knowing him who has called us by name and invited us to come to him through a glorious manifestation of his goodness.*
> *—2 Peter 1:2–3(TPT)*

In the kingdom, what you know is more valuable than what you feel. I don't advocate ignoring your feelings. I'm merely informing you not to be subject to them. The only thing that should move you is the Word of God. Whether you hear His voice audibly, discern it by reading Scripture, or simply experience a knowing inside you, value His spoken word above everything else. I've learned for myself that His voice is irresistible. I'm a witness. You can walk through any storm with Him—just as Peter walked on the water in Matthew 14:27–29. Faith in God can override any of the natural laws of creation.

When you know God is on your side, you become confident. You become strong and courageous despite the odds, regardless of the foe, trusting in God's abilities and in His will for your life. Cancer is no match for your faith. Faith will cleanse your blood. High blood pressure is subject to faith. Strokes are powerless against the Word in you. Heart and kidney disease are no match for the treasure hidden in these earthen vessels. Divorce, bankruptcy, loneliness, unemployment, debt, relationship issues are all subservient to the precious faith you possess.

## *The Source of Confidence*

You may be wondering how I can be so sure when you saw the MRI results. You feel the pressure. You heard what the doctor said. Every part of you wants to worry and give up. You received the bad report in the mail. The checkbook is telling you what can't be done. You feel the pain. He left you. They lied to you. The judge ruled against you.

In my twelve years of pastoring, I've heard just about everything. *But God!*

> While we look not at the things which are seen, but at the things which are not seen: for the things which are seen are temporal; but the things which are not seen are eternal.
> **—2 Corinthians 4:18**

You just read the source of my confidence. This verse breathes a radical form of courage and strength deep in my soul. I believe it is doing the same inside you.

The devil is looking for a reaction. He doesn't know

what's working. He can't read your mind. He needs to stimulate your receptors. He can only work through what you can see, hear, taste, touch, or feel. However, we have an infinite advantage. We don't live by our senses—we live by faith. Your faith doesn't need to consult with your physical receptors. It draws from the unseen realm where there are no limits.

Is your faith based on what God has done for you, or is it based on your love for Him? I pray it is the latter. Reserve your faith for God only, not for the things He does. Thank Him for what He does, but reserve your faith for who He is in your life. This way your faith won't falter when things don't go according to plan. Your faith will still flourish because it's rooted in Him, not in the things He does. Your faith is reserved for God alone. Therefore, your confidence is well suited for Him.

Job's faith was based on his reverence for God and nothing more:

> *Then Job arose, and rent his mantle, and shaved his head, and fell down upon the ground, and worshipped, And said, Naked came I out of my mother's womb, and naked shall I return thither: the LORD gave, and the LORD hath taken away; blessed be the name of the LORD. In all this Job sinned not, nor charged God foolishly.*
> *—Job 1:20–22*

Let's examine another example of confidence in God through the story of the prophet Elisha. In 2 Kings 6:15–17, the servant of Elisha woke up and saw an enormous enemy army surrounding the city. The enemy had chariots, which represented the most fearsome weapon of the time. The servant didn't see a way out. He envisioned doom and destruction.

How do you handle the unexpected? What is your first

reaction when doom and destruction oppose you? Satan often uses sudden terror to instill fear. This is the same spirit of terrorism we see in the world today. Faith doesn't work in tandem with fear. Fear is faith in your problem. Don't fear. God has not given you the spirit of fear (2 Timothy 1:7). Fear is a spirit, which means it cannot be destroyed. Fear is always present. You must resist fear in order for faith to function.

The devil brought everything to bear against Elisha. He used the military tactic of shock and awe to try to intimidate Elisha. It didn't work. Examine Elisha's response to his servant in verse 16: "And he answered, Fear not: for they that be with us are more than they that be with them."

In other words, "Don't be afraid, be confident like me. I put my faith in an unseen God who rules in an unseen world, and this enemy is no match for the supernatural forces on our side."

Then Elisha prayed to God to give his servant permission to see what Elisha saw. According to 2 Kings 6:17:

> Elisha prayed, and said, LORD, I pray thee, open his eyes, that he may see. And the LORD opened the eyes of the young man; and he saw: and, behold, the mountain was full of horses and chariots of fire round about Elisha.

The servant had natural eyes that were limited to a natural way of seeing and, thereby, thinking. Common sense perceived pending destruction. This opened the door for the spirit of fear to come in and the spirit of faith to vacate.

However, Elisha reveals another set of eyes: the eyes of the Spirit. He prayed for God to open the servant's spiritual eyes. Your spirit has eyes that are designed to empower you to see as God sees. How does God see? He sees what He has spoken. Train your mind to yield to your spirit by studying God's Word. Secondly, notice the forces of heaven were surrounding Elisha, not the city. You have an abundance of angelic support and protection.

My friend, have faith in God. I've made this statement multiple times in different ways, so you won't shipwreck your faith. Be confident in God and His power.

CHAPTER ELEVEN

# Ears to Hear

Give Jesus and His Word your complete attention. I have discovered fixation on Him is the key to unlocking unlimited potential for the supernatural.

You're not like most people. Most people fixate their energy trying to get things to work out satisfactorily. They spend most of their prayer time trying to convince God to deliver them out of some problem. They violate their covenant of grace, blame the devil for it, and plead with God to save them. When their prayers aren't answered due to unbelief, they spend their waking hours trying to figure out what to do next.

You're different. Your approach is different. You possess a mouth trained to speak things that are not as though they are. You see yourself through His righteousness. You have an ear that is fine-tuned to God's voice. You know God has something to say to you. You're prepared to wait on God if the answer doesn't come right away. You cast down all the thoughts of Satan that come into your mind. By watching what you say, you don't give the devil the pleasure of knowing if anything he's trying to do is working. You control your emotions by thinking on things that are lovely and uplifting. You create a confession that articulates what you believe and the expected outcome. Your confidence is growing as the pressure from circumstances is mounting.

Despite what I just said, there are times or seasons in our lives when we feel overwhelmed or mentally exhausted. Sometimes it's not one thing in particular but a series of events, one storm after another. At other times, it could be a major setback or a catastrophic event. Whatever the case, I believe the trials of today require more faith than the trials of yesterday.

Where do you get the strength to overcome this newest foe? You need the supernatural power of God. You need to see the manifestation of His presence, the power of God that dwells within the spirit of every born-again believer. One demonstration of His power can start a revolution.

## *It Starts with a Word*

In Matthew 14, we see the story of Jesus sending the disciples across the lake while He stays behind to pray. This account is better known by what happens next: Jesus walks on the water, and Peter joins Him.

Every assignment starts with a word from God. The Bible says, "in the beginning was the Word" (John 1:1). In this story, the word from Jesus was, "Let's go to the other side." Everything starts and ends with a word from God spoken directly to you. It's a rhema word that contains the power for fulfillment of the assignment.

While the written Word—the logos—is for everyone, the rhema word is designed specifically for you. His rhema word will provide the clarity and provision that's needed for your journey. First Kings 17:2–4 says Elijah received a word from God to get to the brook Cherith, where God had assigned ravens to provide for Elijah. Always look to what God is saying or has said to you. If you're not sure, do what Jesus did in Matthew 14:

*And straightway Jesus constrained his disciples to get into a ship, and to go before him unto the other side, while he sent the multitudes away. And when he had sent the multitudes away, he went up into a mountain apart to pray: and when the evening was come, he was there alone.*
*—Matthew 14:22-23*

Remove every distraction, and spend time alone with God to receive from Him. There are times when you have to lock yourself away in order to quiet your spirit so you can hear His voice.

He knows you. He knows the best way to reveal His mind to you. It might be an audible voice or an inner voice that exudes confidence. To others it may come through personal study of the Word. Most believers can relate to the moment the words leap off the page of the Bible, and in that instant you know. Exactly how God chooses to reveal something is not the issue. What matters is that you have faith God will speak to you in a way you can comprehend Him. Remember, God will always reward pursuit. Your responsibility is to believe to receive.

Satan specializes in background noise. Jesus said to go to the other side. The storm was the background noise that Satan conjured up to keep the disciples from focusing on what Jesus said. We've all experienced situations out in public when you receive an important phone call, but you can't hear the person on the phone because of all the noise in the background. The remedy is to find a quiet place to hear. You need to regularly find a quiet place to hear from God, a place free from all the noise of life and the confusion of the world.

## *Hear His Voice*

I believe the greatest attribute of any believer is his or her ability to hear from God. Hearing God's voice clearly takes the stress out of life. Hearing that is free from Satan's static is the difference between confidence and confusion. There is something reassuring when you know that you've heard from God.

I strongly recommend you repent of any sins in your life as you pursue God. Sin will disrupt your communication with the Father. If you're finding it difficult to hear from God, often the reason is unrepentant sin. Humble yourself before Him. Ask God to forgive you for anything you've done knowingly or unknowingly. He will forgive you. With the confidence of knowing that He heard you, pursue the Father with all your heart: "And ye shall seek me, and find me, when ye shall search for me with all your heart" (Jeremiah 29:13).

Furthermore, I want to demystify God's ability to speak to you. What I mean is, I want to challenge the Old Testament archetypes that many believers falsely see as God's primary means of communicating with them. Read Hebrews 1:1–2 carefully:

*God, who at sundry times and in divers manners spake in time past unto the fathers by the prophets, Hath in these last days spoken unto us by his Son, whom he hath appointed heir of all things, by whom also he made the worlds..*

This means that God spoke to people using unique forms of communication at specific times. After Adam's transgression, God spoke to men from the outside in. He spoke to Moses through a burning bush (Exodus 3:4). Then He spoke to Moses in the wilderness at the door of the tabernacle (Exodus 29:42). Throughout the Old Testament, God used unique ways at specific times to speak to His people.

However, Hebrews 1:2 informs us that God changed

His way of communicating with mankind. Why? Because there has been a change in relationship: we are *children* of God in this age, compared to *servants* of God in the Old Testament. Now God speaks to us directly through Jesus. We no longer require an intermediary. God speaks directly to you, and Jesus is the One who made it possible. You now have the ability to hear God's voice for yourself. We now hear God's voice from the inside. Jesus tells His hearers throughout His earthly ministry: "He that hath ears to hear, let him hear" (Matthew 11:15).

You need to utilize the ears of your spirit so you can discern the voice of God for yourself. Hearing God speak to you is crucial for your success in life. He knows how to get His point across. God knows how to get your attention.

I believe He's speaking to you as you read this book. The question is, do you have an ear to hear? Don't blame God for not speaking. We get so tied up in day-to-day issues of life that we don't take the time to cultivate our relationship with Him. Time with God is an afterthought for many. For many, we are only aware of our need for Him when we get in trouble.

Jesus made it a point to spend time with His Father daily, early in the morning. David said, "Early will I seek thee" (Psalm 63:1). Put first things first. Make communication with God your first priority every day. God promises a reward to those who have their priorities in order. Jesus said, "But seek ye first the kingdom of God, and his righteousness; and all these things shall be added unto you" (Matthew 6:33).

## *In Spirit and in Truth*

Trusting God requires a formal divorce from reliance on your five senses. These senses are vital in a natural world and serve as a means of protection, awareness, and function. However, the real you is spirit, and the spirit functions at a much higher level of existence than the body. The spirit is eternal and feeds on the eternal things of God. To limit yourself to what is possible naturally is to deny yourself of your full spiritual potential. God is spirit and He requires us to come up to where He is, and not the other way around.

Recall the words of Jesus:

*But the hour cometh, and now is, when the true worshippers shall worship the Father in spirit and in truth: for the Father seeketh such to worship him. God is a Spirit: and they that worship him must worship him in spirit and in truth.*

*—John 4:23–24*

God seeks worship on His terms: in spirit and in truth. He expects us to approach Him through the indwelling Spirit of truth that lives within us. Any other means is rejected. Our communication with God is only possible through the Holy Spirit, who aids us through intercession and spiritual expressions that the human language cannot articulate (Romans 8:26).

This is what makes speaking in tongues so vital in your communication with God. Speaking in tongues is not an event reserved for the early church that expired over time. It is not outdated or old-fashioned. Speaking in tongues is vital for you to communicate with God on His terms—in spirit and in truth. It is Spirit calling upon spirit and deep calling upon deep (Psalm 42:7).

It is only by the Spirit of God that you can truly experience the fullness of God in your life. When you speak in tongues, you are praying in the spirit realm. The natural part of you is temporarily disengaged, and the real you prays to God through your spirit, outside of natural restrictions. Your mind is not involved. Your spirit engages God on His terms. It's you and God. The Holy Spirit helps you every step of the way with groanings that cannot be uttered or duplicated. Praying in tongues is praying in truth.

Don't be shocked if all your anxieties disappear after you've prayed in tongues. Praying in tongues unleashes God's boldness in you. All fear is brushed aside and in its place is an expectation of the supernatural power of God.

I believe speaking in tongues is the earthly proof that a believer has experienced the Holy Spirit baptism:

> *And they of the circumcision which believed were astonished, as many as came with Peter, because that on the Gentiles also was poured out the gift of the Holy Ghost. For they heard them speak with tongues, and magnify God.*
> *—Acts 10:45-46*

While the Holy Spirit baptism is not essential for salvation, it is vital if you want to live a truly victorious life in Christ.

Furthermore, I believe if you want to know what Adam lost in the beginning, simply look at what Jesus restored. I believe Adam lost the gift of speaking in tongues.

Look at what Jesus said the disciples would be given in order to be His witnesses throughout the earth (Acts 1:8): "And, behold, I send the promise of my Father upon you: but tarry ye in the city of Jerusalem, until ye be endued with power from on high" (Luke 24:49).

Jesus restored the power of the Holy Spirit into humanity. Now, when we repent of our sins and ask Jesus to come into our hearts, we are born again. The Holy Spirit comes into our hearts in that instant, and our names are written in the Lamb's book of life (Revelation 21:27). Now we can also receive the promise of the Father, the Holy Spirit baptism. This baptism is received by the same faith it took to become born again. You believe the promise, then ask God to fill you. You can be filled anytime and anywhere. For most, it happens when a minister lays hands on them. But you can be filled at home by yourself. Simply ask God to fill you and receive.

*If ye then, being evil, know how to give good gifts unto your children: how much more shall your heavenly Father give the Holy Spirit to them that ask him?*
**—Luke 11:13**

Open your mouth and speak by faith. Let the language come out of your spirit. Understanding is not a prerequisite. Just speak no matter what it sounds like, and speak by faith. Having received, now listen for God's voice. And remember, it's His good pleasure to give you the kingdom.

CONCLUSION

# Right Words

*The Lord GOD hath given me the tongue of the learned, that
I should know how to speak a word in season to him that
is weary: he wakeneth morning by morning, he wakeneth
mine ear to hear as the learned.*

***—Isaiah 50:4***

How precious is a word spoken in season? I pray the
words God has given me for this book are forceable words
in your life (Job 6:25). My prayer is that they are words
spoken in season that speak to your need or enhance your
understanding of the Scriptures. I trust each scripture drew
you closer to God and each chapter revealed an applicable
truth that takes your relationship with Jesus to another
level of faith and intimacy.

I've spoken from experience. I bear the scars of
carrying my cross daily and fighting through many of the
same challenges you have faced or will face. The good
news is that we win. The victory has been summed up in
Christ who lives and abides forever, of whose kingdom
there is no end.

I pray the pitfalls of religion and the need for a more
intimate relationship with Jesus will be more apparent to

you after having read this book. Run this race called life that you might obtain the prize.

*Know ye not that they which run in a race run all, but one receiveth the prize? So run, that ye may obtain.*
**—1 Corinthians 9:24**

Live your life with zeal for God. You only get one life on earth. Value the opportunity that God has given you. Don't waste time on things that don't support your purpose for living. Treat time as a currency. Time is far too precious to waste.

## *Be Born Again*

With this in mind, I won't make the mistake of assuming everyone who reads this book is born again. Or maybe you're in a backslidden state. Come home to God today. If you don't know Jesus, if you've never made a conscious decision to receive His sacrifice for your sins, make the decision today to receive salvation. Heaven is waiting on your arrival.

Life is short. You must be born again! If this request is stirring in your heart, read out loud and believe in your heart the following prayer:

Heavenly Father, I come to You in the Name of Jesus. Your Word says whosoever shall call on the name of Jesus shall be saved. I am calling on you today.

I ask you Jesus to come into my heart and be Lord over my life according to Romans 10:9–10: "If thou shalt confess with thy mouth the Lord Jesus, and shalt believe in thine heart that God hath raised him from the dead, thou shalt be saved. For with the heart man believeth unto righteousness; and with the mouth confession is made unto salvation."

I do this now. I confess that Jesus is Lord. I believe that God raised Him from the dead. I am now born again. Thank you, Jesus, for saving me. Amen!

Halleluiah, you are now born again! You are no longer a sinner but a saint, and there's more to be had. Ask God to baptize you in the Holy Spirit. When you ask, believe you receive, open your mouth, and speak.

Now ask God to lead you to a Bible-believing church. Submit yourself to its leadership, get water-baptized with understanding, and watch the power of God transform your life. Amen and amen!

APPENDIX A

# A Simplified Overview of the Holy Scriptures

God decides to extend His kingdom rulership from heaven onto a small planet called Earth.

God decides to share His rulership mandate with man, whom He created in His own image and likeness, to spread kingdom living on the earth.

God puts man in charge of the earth and gives him a kingdom mandate to transfer heaven's culture to the earth, but retains ownership for Himself.

Man sins, losing the kingdom of God, and transfers rulership to a fallen angel named Satan, who by proxy becomes the god of this world.

God announces a coming Messiah and kingdom restoration, tells Satan what the Messiah will do to him, sentences Satan to eternal damnation, and gives him four thousand years before his damnation to the lake of fire.

God creates a prototype of the church called Israel to show the world what the kingdom of heaven is like.

Through the law of Moses, God prepares humanity for the reintroduction of the kingdom man lost.

God sends the prophets to testify about the coming

Messiah and His kingdom.

John the Baptist introduces Jesus as the Messiah and confirms the kingdom of heaven is now at hand.

Jesus preaches the message of the kingdom and manifests the culture of the kingdom by demonstration of supernatural power, signs, wonders, and miracles.

Jesus lays down His life and is raised from the dead by the Father, thereby becoming the door through which the redeemed receive salvation and eternal life. Through Jesus, the redeemed take possession of the kingdom He came from heaven to restore.

Jesus ascends into heaven and sends the Holy Spirit, as comforter, into the earth.

The Holy Spirit's arrival births the church age.

The Holy Spirit is now living inside every believer, perfecting the things of the kingdom that concern us, steadily forming Christ in us.

As sanctioned ambassadors and citizens of the kingdom, we now carry the message of reconciliation that the whole human family is eligible to receive.

We possess the mandate of dominion to spread the kingdom over the entire earth as the waters cover the seas, and, in doing so, we enforce Satan's defeat.

In the meantime, all of creation is groaning with anticipation for the manifestation of the true sons of God, until the rapture of the church, the second advent of Christ, and the eternal establishment of His kingdom on the earth.

The end.

I know I've oversimplified things, but this basic outline should help you with a general understanding of God's plan of restoration and the reestablishment of the kingdom of heaven on earth as it is in heaven. I want you to see the overriding importance of God's kingdom in each of the seventeen aforementioned statements.

This is why the primary message of Jesus is about the kingdom of God!

APPENDIX B

# 100 Lessons from the Life of Abraham

1. Believe God.

2. God can be your only source.

3. Take God at His Word.

4. You can only live successfully by following what is written in God's Word.

5. God will not do what He has not already spoken.

6. Be careful what you give consideration to.

7. Don't take matters into your own hands.

8. Let God be God.

9. A word from God is a word to God.

10. God doesn't need your ability; He needs your faith.

11. Take heed of what voices you listen to.

12. Wait on God.

13. Rehearse what God said to you until it becomes a part of you.

14. There will always be people who don't believe what you believe; accept it.

15. Stick to what God said, not to how things appear.

16. Faith proves circumstances change before they change.

17. When you consider the promise, it will always be too big for your mind.

18. Don't let your mind talk you out of believing God.

19. Faith will require you to use your imagination.

20. See yourself as God sees you.

21. Say what God says about you, not what others say.

22. Fortify your faith.

23. Tough days of testing are coming; you can't avoid them.

24. Testing is always a prerequisite of faith.

25. Follow Abraham's example of faith.

26. Say what you believe.

27. Keep saying what you believe until you truly believe it.

28. You cannot possess what you refuse to say.

29. The devil will try to make you ashamed of what you're believing God for.

30. Faith demands you live solely by what is written.

31. Faith is God's will for you.

32. Create faith images in your mind to keep you motivated.

33. When you don't know what to do, stand; don't stagger.

34. You know your faith is working when it looks like nothing is working.

35. Faith itself is proof you have what you desire.

36. Faith is the proof heaven respects.

37. Faith has no regard for age.

38. God doesn't care how old or young you are, and neither should you.

39. Faith ensures angelic support.

40. Faith works when you're not working.

41. Faith starts where your ability ends.

42. Use faith for everything, not just in times of trouble or need.

43. Faith is the assurance of the promise.

44. God will never ask you to do something you can do on your own.

45. God will never command you to do something you cannot do.

46. Faith sees the end from the beginning.

47. Faith starts when you stop.

48. If you can make it happen, you don't need faith.

49. God makes Himself essential for the fulfillment of the promise.

50. Whatever God asks you to do will require faith.

51. You don't know what you believe until it's tested.

52. Tested faith is real faith.

53. Untested faith is fake.

54. Consider God's ability, not yours.

55. Know that God is a quickening spirit.

56. God has all the power you need.

57. Imagine the impossible.

58. Think the impossible.

59. Speak the impossible.

60. Decide to be strong in faith; it's a choice.

61. Resist the temptation to try to figure things out.

62. Remember God knows things you don't know.

63. God will never tell you everything.

64. God only tells you the outcome; you have to believe through the journey.

65. Learn to love the notion of believing God.

66. Hate the notion of unbelief.

67. Your faith came from God; all unbelief comes from the devil.

68. Unbelief is the devil's alternative to faith.

69. Satan rewards people for their unbelief.

70. Unbelief is simply faith in the devil's kingdom.

71. Believe that you possess what's needed to get the job done.

72. Faith is always rewarded.

73. Expect God to reward you.

74. Your faith brings glory to God.

75. Faith proves you have confidence in God's kingdom.

76. It's not faith if you don't need God.

77. In faith you have mastery over your circumstances.

78. In unbelief your circumstances will master you.

79. Convince yourself that God cannot lie.

80. Faith calls things into existence.

81. Faith brings manifestation of any promise.

82. Faith has no respect for problems.

83. Faith draws from heaven.

84. Faith proves what you're believing exists.

85. Faith doesn't consult the natural to prove the supernatural.

86. Faith specializes in the impossible.

87. Faith works on God's timing.

88. Faith does not work according to man's timing.

89. Faith will lie dormant if you don't use it.

90. Faith is a law.

91. Faith is a spirit.

92. You will need patience in your walk of faith.

93. You live by faith, day by day.

94. You cannot run by faith.

95. You must learn to walk by faith.

96. It's clear that God enjoys you living by faith.

97. God enjoys the fulfillment of His promises in your life more than you enjoy receiving from Him.

98. Faith is always tied to a promise.

99. Get to know God's promises intimately.

100. The Bible is your only book reference for faith.

# About the Author

Pastor Anthony S. Ramsey is founder and senior pastor of the Kingdom Living Church of Grand Blanc, Michigan. His passion for the advancement of the kingdom of God has resulted in thousands receiving salvation and in numerous miracles, signs, and wonders since Kingdom Living's inception in 2007.

Anthony's anointing as a powerful, practical kingdom teacher has resulted in countless proofs of the power of the kingdom, as individuals and families alike have experienced supernatural transformations spiritually, physically, and financially.

God has honored him to take the transformative message of the kingdom into the local jail system, regional prison, homeless shelter, and women's shelter, where he and his staff minister seven services per month.

Prior to receiving his pastoral ordination through the "laying on of hands" by his bishop and spiritual father, Bishop Andrew Merritt of the Straight Gate International Church of Detroit, Michigan, he served as an automotive executive for over 25 years, which culminated in his last position as CEO of a $16 million automotive supplier.

Anthony is married to Marvella and is the father of four children: Blake, Rosston, Ria Cymone', and Roman.

The motto and mission at KLC is "Kingdom Living Church, where it's not about Religion but Relationship." This Holy Spirit-inspired mantra is the platform by which Pastor Ramsey boldly declares the transformative force of faith.

REFERENCES

# Notes

[1] *Dictionary.com,* "danger." Based on Random House Unabridged Dictionary. Random House, 2020. https://www.dictionary.com/browse/danger?s=t.

[2] *Lexico,* "religion." https://www.lexico.com/en/definition/religion.

[3] *Merriam-Webster,* "tare." https://www.merriam-webster.com/dictionary/tare.

[4] *Lexico,* "religion." https://www.lexico.com/en/definition/religion.

[5] Marcy, William Learned. Quoted in Gregory Titelman. *Random House Dictionary of Popular Proverbs and Sayings.* Random House, 1996.

[6] *Merriam-Webster,* "husbandman." https://www.merriam-webster.com/dictionary/husbandman.

[7] Strong, James. "H430: Elohiym." *A Concise Dictionary of the Words in the Greek Testament and The Hebrew Bible*. Faithlife, 2019.

[8] Virkler, Mark. "The Real Difference Between Logos and Rhema Words." Charisma News. October 5, 2018. https://www.charismanews.com/opinion/73604-the-real-difference-between-logos-and-rhema-words.

[9] *Lexico*, "exploit." https://www.lexico.com/definition/exploit.

[10] *Dictionary.com*, "diligent." Based on Random House Unabridged Dictionary. Random House, 2020. https://www.dictionary.com/browse/diligent.

[11] Merritt, Andrew. *My Faith Is Taking Me Someplace: Are You on the Road to Nowhere?* 2nd edition. Charisma House, 1997.

[12] *Dictionary.com*, "theocracy." Based on Random House Unabridged Dictionary. Random House, 2020. https://www.dictionary.com/browse/theocracy.

[13] Strong, James. *Strong's Exhaustive Concordance of the Bible*. Abingdon Press, 1890.

Made in the USA
Monee, IL
25 October 2020